Livia
McRee

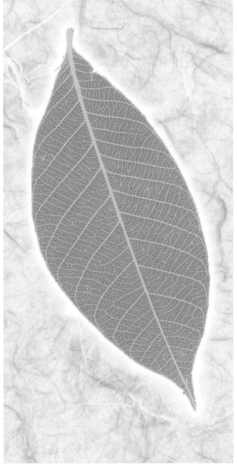

Instant
Fabric

Quilted

Projects

from Your

Home

Computer

Martingale
& COMPANY

BOTHELL, WASHINGTON

Credits

President .... Nancy J. Martin
CEO .... Daniel J. Martin
Publisher .... Jane Hamada
Editorial Director .... Mary V. Green
Editorial Project Manager .... Tina Cook
Technical Editor .... Dawn Anderson
Copy Editors ... Lily G. Casura & Leslie Phillips
Design and Production Manager ..... Stan Green
Illustrator .... Laurel Strand
Photographer .... Brent Kane
Cover and Text Designer .... Stan Green

That Patchwork Place is an imprint of
Martingale & Company.

Instant Fabric: Quilted Projects from
Your Home Computer
© 2000 by Livia McRee

Martingale & Company
PO Box 118
Bothell, WA 98041-0118 USA
www.patchwork.com

Printed in Hong Kong

05 04 03 02 01 00   6 5 4 3 2 1

Dedication

This book is lovingly dedicated to my Mother
and my Mima—two wonderful women.

Acknowledgments

I would like to thank Biz Stone for contributing
his beautiful artwork to this book, as well as for
his support and inspiration.

Library of Congress Cataloging-in-Publication Data

McRee, Livia.
    Instant fabric : quilted projects from your home
computer / Livia McRee.
        p. cm.
    ISBN 1-56477-348-5
    1. Patchwork—Patterns. 2. Quilting. I. Title.

    TT835 .M255 2000
    746.46'041'0285—dc21   00-064747

Mission Statement

We are dedicated to providing quality products
and service by working together to inspire
creativity and to enrich the lives we touch.

CONTENTS

INTRODUCTION

The projects in this book are intended to take you a step further than straightforward image transferring. Using your computer, a scanner, an inkjet color printer, and some image-editing software, you'll be able to expand your creativity as far as you want to go!

It used to be that a scanner and printer, especially a color printer, were high-priced wonder machines available to only a select few because of their tremendous cost. But now, you can buy a scanner for as little as $75, and an inkjet printer for as little as $150. A color printer will more than pay for itself if you plan on making lots of color copies for some of your projects, because this can get expensive when done at a copy shop.

Another tool you'll need is image-editing software. If your computer didn't come with a simplified image-editing program, you have several low-cost options. Some of these programs are very simple, but others, intended for use by graphic artists, are complicated and have a wide range of extraordinary capabilities, with an equally steep learning curve for mastering them. Perhaps the best-known program in this market is Adobe's PhotoShop, frequently used by professionals and priced at several hundred dollars. A little-known fact, however, is that Adobe also offers a "limited edition" of Photo-Shop for around $100, whose features allow for lots of flexibility. An added bonus is that if you plan on buying a scanner, you might find that it comes with an image-editing software package of its own. Compare before you buy: you just might find excellent image-editing software bundled with your scanner for no additional cost.

Finally, the most important thing to remember when learning to produce artwork on your computer is not to be afraid of the process. Don't be afraid to make mistakes or worry about "messing things up." One of the best things about computers is their ability to do something over, with little effort on your part. Remember, by using a computer you'll be able to save hours and hours of cutting and pasting by hand. So, feel free to experiment, relax, and enjoy!

PREPARING ARTWORK

In this book, the projects I've chosen use "copyright free" art. This is art that's in the public domain, and on which no copyright applies, unlike almost all other creative works.

About the Artwork

Publishers like Dover Books produce hundreds of books filled with copyright-free artwork, often called "clip art," for artists and craftspeople to use in their projects. Some restrictions still can apply. For example, Dover gives permission for people to use up to ten illustrations from each of their books in a project if the project appears in a publication. Other artists and publishers might give you permission to use a piece of artwork in an item you're making for your personal use, but restrict that right if you were going to sell or display the item commercially. Be sure to check with the original artist or publisher first: it's not just courteous, it's the law. But if you want to stay on the safe side, use copyright-free artwork, specifically designated by its publishers as such, as I have for the projects in this book. (See "Sources"). When in doubt, be sure to ask permission, and get it in writing.

One great benefit of using material such as that mentioned in the "Sources" section (from Dover or Shambhala) is that it's often on CD-ROM, as well as in book form. Having the clip art on CD-ROM eliminates the need for scanning the artwork and cuts back significantly on the time it takes to make these projects.

Some artwork has been specifically created for this book. This artwork is available for personal use, free of charge.

About the Printer Fabric

The June Tailor printer fabric used in this book is an extraordinary product. There are, however, some key things to keep in mind when working with it. Before printing for the first time on any piece of the fabric, run your hands lightly along the surface of the fabric to make sure it's free of lint and bumps. If you find any, carefully remove them with your fingers. Otherwise, they'll be sure to come off during the washing process, leaving your printed fabric with one or more bright white spots.

Another thing to keep in mind is that the color that your fabric prints out will be somewhat different from what you see on your computer screen (usually, lighter). Normally this isn't a problem, as colors darken a little after the printer fabric is rinsed. However, if you are fastidious about needing the color to be exactly right, you may want to try adjusting the color and testing your work first on pieces of paper.

Once you print your design on the fabric sheet, let the sheet dry overnight. Then rinse the fabric in a sink full of cold water to make it colorfast. Don't skip this step, even if you don't expect the finished product to ever be washed. The danger is that without this step, the smallest amount of moisture could ruin your hard work. So gently submerge the printed fabric and swirl it around for several seconds. When you remove the fabric from the water, have a dry, absorbent towel at the ready, and press the fabric between the layers of this towel. Squeeze out all the excess water, then lay the sheet flat to dry. This helps prevent color bleeding, which can be especially bad if there is type on your fabric. The fabric will also shrink anywhere from $\frac{1}{8}$" to $\frac{1}{2}$" so it's crucial to measure the fabric as you cut it, rather than depending on the image for sizing.

Another consideration is how best to quilt your finished piece, whether by machine or by hand. Because printer fabric is thicker than normal cotton, and also resistant to punctures by needles and pins; I recommend glue basting wherever possible, and machine quilting.

THE TECHNOLOGY

Using a Scanner

Before using your scanner for the first time, be sure to thoroughly read the manual that came with it, and follow the recommendations it makes for optimizing the quality of your scanned images. You'll need to let the scanner know how big an image you're working with, how high a quality of resolution to use when scanning it, and whether your image is color, or black and white. Results will vary widely, depending on the settings you choose. A scanner's resolution refers to how many "dots per inch" ("dpi") characterize each scan. As with printed material, the higher the dpi, the greater the image density and often the clarity as well. Experiment and see for yourself how changing the dpi varies the quality of the scan you make. Black and white line art can be scanned at a much lower resolution than full-color photos where you want to capture every detail, but bear in mind that it's also possible to go overboard. Higher resolution scans mean larger (sometimes gigantic) image files, and these can significantly slow down your computer and printer. For the projects in this book, a resolution of 150 dpi is sufficient. Resolutions any higher than that will likely bog down your system's performance and significantly slow down the time it takes you to do a project.

Tip: If you find that your computer's performance gets sluggish once you start collecting a few large scans on your desktop, try "off loading" the scans onto high-capacity storage media, like the popular ZIP disk. Often you can use a single ZIP disk to store a number of scanned images, at various resolutions, and leave the performance of your system otherwise intact.

Image-Editing Software

The best bet for learning what your image-editing software is able to do is to explore the manual that came with it. Each software package varies greatly, and the manufacturer can help you understand best how to work with the software you have.

Some general hints for working with images, however, are the following:

- Image-editing software often allows you to view your images in pixels, inches, or centimeters. Pixels are the tiny dots that, grouped together, comprise your image. The more dots you have per square inch, the more detailed your picture will be. So if you are printing a document that is 150 dots per inch (dpi), your printer is putting 150 dots of color (or grays) in every inch of your image. Choose "inches" as your measurement—that will make it easier to follow the directions in this book.

- When copying and pasting images from one document to another, be sure the dpi of every document you're working with is the same. If they're different, the images will look either too big or too small. For example, if you were to paste a 300 dpi flower into a background document that was only 150 dpi, the flower would be twice the size you expected! This problem is easy to fix, though. You should have a setting that allows you to change the dpi easily; simply change each document to the desired dpi before you copy and paste.

- When you're working on a project, and manipulating the image differently for different effects, it helps to save the scans under slightly different names (leaf1, leaf2, leaf3) to differentiate them. When you have several versions of the same thing handy, you're more likely to feel free to experiment with them than to worry about "wrecking" your one and only good copy of an image.

- Be sure to conserve your work by saving image files frequently, in case your computer crashes. (When your computer starts slowing down—or even before—is the perfect time to start moving your image files onto high-capacity storage disks, like ZIP disks.

- When you're ready to play with the capabilities of your software, try rotating the image or changing its size. You may also be able to lighten or brighten the image, change it from black and white to color or vice versa, sharpen it or blur it, or change the amount of contrast (helpful when a scanned image seems to come out too dark). You can also tweak the colors of the image or the background, and "improve" them, or even change them altogether. Sometimes you may want to just "erase" an unwanted area of the scanned image, and you can do this as well. You can also reduce or enlarge the size of the image, or change the amount of background around the image. Play around with the software, its selection tools, and a sample image, and learn how much range the software really has.

- When you work with detailed pictures such as the flowers in the "Floral Bolster Pillow" project, you may have trouble filling in all the background areas of your image, especially within the flowers' petals and leaves. Sensitive scans can pick up barely discernible details in a seemingly simple image. Adjusting the contrast or brightening the image will drop out unwanted subtleties and help clean up the image, making it more workable.

- With many of the projects in this book, you'll be creating a background color for the image to appear against. You can use software to do this, by selecting the area to be filled and using the program's color palette to fill the space you've selected. With some programs, you can use a tool to select a color that already exists in the spectrum of colors in the image that you've scanned. This can be very helpful. There's also an interesting effect called "screening back," where you can use only a percentage of a color to fill another area, resulting in a more translucent appearance. There are many ways to select a particular area of an image to modify, and a number of different effects that are possible. Let your creativity have free rein, and see what results.

Throughout, I will give instructions for the projects two ways: using a scanner and computer, and using a color copier. Look for sections entitled, "Preparing the Artwork with a Computer, Scanner, and Printer" and "Preparing the Artwork with a Photocopier."

Printing

While you're getting ready to print a specific image and its background, you'll probably want to include what's known as bleed—an area beyond the edge of the image into which the colors extend. This gives you the crucial margin for error for the seam allowance, so that you don't accidentally find an edge of white fabric peeking through your finished work. You may also find yourself dipping into this "extra" if your fabric shrinks too much after washing.

To ensure the desired area of bleed, select the artwork and copy and paste it into a space that's bigger by ½" all around. Select a color for the image's bleed that closely matches the color at your image's edges. It helps if it's slightly different, so you can tell where the image ends and the bleed begins.

Before printing your image on the fabric, do a test run on paper first until you are satisfied with the results. To print, check your work first in the "printer preview" or "page setup" in your software, and select the orientation of your printed image, whether "portrait" (vertical) or "landscape" (horizontal) format. If everything looks good, set the printer resolution on "high" and print on paper. If you like the result, go immediately to fabric. (Taking this extra step will cut down on waste and expense, saving the printer fabric for final versions only.)

Using a Color Photocopier

If you're going to use a color photocopier for your image transfers, be sure to take the package of printer fabric sheets and its instructions to the copy store for the clerk to read, to make sure they have the appropriate machines available. (Many expensive copy machines are not self-service.) Here, too, since color copying mistakes can become expensive, it pays to do all your design prep work in black and white, such as determining percentages of the area to be printed, and so on. Once you've got these set, go ahead and get the color copies made.

T i p : A couple projects in this book, the Shell Wall Hanging and the Floral Bolster Pillow, involve colorizing black-and-white art. If your local copy shop can't accommodate you, try hand-coloring the images with pencils. You just need to make a clear black-and-white copy and use a light touch with the pencils to achieve a tinted look.

QUILTING BASICS

Fabric

I recommend using 100 percent cotton fabric for all the projects in this book. It's easy to handle, easy to quilt, and gives reliable results. The "Sources" section at the back of this book provides contact information for several excellent companies that specialize in 100 percent cotton fabric especially for quilters. Always preshrink new fabrics by machine washing and drying, even when making a project that won't be washed—such as a wall hanging—to remove the residual chemicals left on the fabric from the factory. Then press the fabric before cutting to ensure accurate measurements and prevent fabric warp.

Supplies

SEWING MACHINE

The projects in this book are quilted almost entirely by machine, because printer fabric is difficult to quilt by hand. Machine quilting needles are also helpful because they make smaller puncture holes in the fabric than standard sewing needles, which results in a nicer finish.

THREAD

High quality quilting thread—thread which is made especially for quilting, and is thick and strong—is important. I used Sulky thread for several of the projects in this book. It's shinier than cotton thread, and even comes in spools of variegated color, which can add another dimension to the look of your finished product.

TOOLS

You will need good, sharp scissors, template-making material such as cardboard and clear template plastic, and an assortment of pins (straight and safety) for basting the layers of the quilt, etc. For cutting your fabric, a rotary cutter, cutting mat, and a 6" x 24" clear acrylic ruler make the job much faster, easier, and more accurate than cutting with scissors. Glue sticks can be used in place of pins or a basting stitch on smaller projects. Air-soluble marking pens are great for transferring quilt patterns. The ink fades over a period of a few days, or it can be removed with a damp sponge; but to be on the safe side, test the pen first on a fabric scrap from your project, just to make sure it doesn't stain.

Rotary Cutting

Your fabric has been washed, dried, and pressed. Now you're ready to prepare it for cutting.

1. Fold the fabric and match selvages, the tightly woven edges of the fabric where the manufacturer's name is often printed. Align the crosswise and lengthwise grains as much

as possible—cutting along the straight of grain will minimize distortion when you sew.

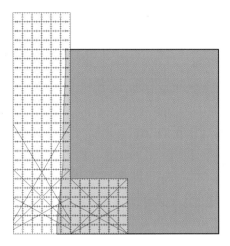

2. Align a square acrylic ruler with the folded edge of fabric, then place a long, straight ruler to the left of the square ruler, just covering the uneven raw edges of the left side of the fabric. Remove the square ruler and cut along the right edge of the long ruler, rolling the rotary cutter away from you. Discard this strip.

3. To cut strips, you don't even need to mark your fabric. Just align the proper measurement on the ruler with the cut edge of the fabric, and then cut along the right side of the ruler. For example, to cut a 2"-wide strip, you'd place the ruler's 2" marking at the edge of the fabric.

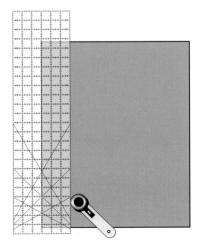

4. To cut squares and rectangles, cut strips of the required width and then remove the selvage ends from the strip. Align the proper ruler measurement with the left edge of the strip and then cut a square or rectangle.

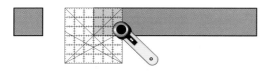

Piecing and Pressing

All the projects in this book call for ¼" seam allowances; when piecing your quilt tops, it's important to maintain this measurement consistently, so that your subsequent piecing will match up properly. It's a good idea to check your measurements and make adjustments, if necessary, as you go along, especially when making a larger quilt such as the "Chinese Lap Quilt" on page 24; for a project like this, making sure all your constructed blocks are the same size before you piece them is crucial.

"Pressing" is a fine art in the quilting world, as distinguished from ironing. "Pressing" involves vertical pressure, with no side-to-side motion (that's "ironing," say the purists). Attention to pressing greatly reduces the chance of distorting the fabric at this stage. Typically, quilters press their seams toward one side, usually toward the darker fabric. This is very important when quilting in-the-ditch (see "Machine Quilting" on page 11). When pressing seams between printer fabric and background fabric, always press away from the printer fabric. It's thicker than the cotton you'll be using, and you don't want it to double up on itself. However, when you join two pieces of printer fabric, press the seam open to reduce bulk. Always be sure to press your seams carefully, to keep fabric stretch and distortion to a minimum.

Transferring the Quilting Pattern

There are many methods of transferring quilting patterns. For the projects in this book, I suggest using an air-soluble marking pen because of its accuracy, visibility, and ease of use. However, you should always test the pen on a scrap of the fabric you intend to use, to make sure it can be removed easily.

Many projects use only straight lines for their quilting designs, and these can be measured and marked directly on the projects. But for more complicated patterns, such as that of the "Arabic Tiles Place Mat," on page 12, you'll want to use a different method. Copy the quilting pattern to the appropriate size, then tape it to your work surface. Tape the fabric to be quilted on top, before you layer the batting and backing. The pattern should be visible, but if you have trouble seeing it, use a light box. Or, for small projects, try taping the pattern and fabric to a sunny window. Then trace the design onto the fabric.

Layering and Basting

When a quilt top is assembled, you'll need to add the batting and backing and secure them both before you begin quilting. For some of the smaller projects in this book, I eliminated the backing at this stage. If you are using a backing, lay the backing right side down, smoothing out all the wrinkles in the fabric. (For larger projects, tape the edges of the backing directly to the work surface, such as a large table or a clean floor.) This is the bottom layer of the quilt sandwich. Next, lay the batting down and smooth it out. (Some people let their batting air out a day or two before this step, to soften the folds.) The batting is the middle layer of the sandwich (or for smaller projects in which the backing was eliminated, the batting is the bottom layer). Finally, lay the quilt top right side up, and smooth it out on top of the other two layers (this is the top layer of the sandwich).

For smaller projects, such as the picture frames or sachets you'll find in this book, feel free to secure the layers with a glue stick. But for larger projects, use safety pins to hold the layers together. Starting in the middle of the quilt, place the safety pins about 3" to 4" apart in an evenly distributed pattern, making sure to avoid specific design areas to be quilted.

Machine Quilting

Almost all the quilting done in the projects in this book is machine quilting, because of the resistant nature of the printer fabric. You may want to practice on a fake quilt "sandwich" (say, the size of a potholder) first to get some experience. To quilt straight lines, simply guide the quilt though your machine keeping it smoothed out, but not taut. A walking foot is especially helpful for large projects, as it feeds both the top and bottom layer through the machine evenly, which reduces puckering and shifting of the fabric.

For projects with curved lines, use free-motion quilting. You may want to purchase a quilting hoop, or special quilting gloves, with grippy finger tips, for greater ease in moving the fabric. The free-motion quilting technique involves dropping the sewing machine's feed dogs and attaching a darning foot. You most likely can find the technique under "darning" in your sewing machine's manual. Free-motion quilting also takes some practice. Hold the fabric taut in a quilter's hoop, then move the fabric under the needle, along the lines of the design you have marked. It will take some practice until

you can produce evenly-sized stitches. Try to relax, and move the fabric smoothly under the needle.

For some of the projects in this book, "in-the-ditch" quilting is called for, which simply means quilting closely parallel to the seam lines of your quilt top. When you press the seam allowance to one side, a "ditch" is formed on the side that the seam is pressed away from. This is where you quilt.

Hand Quilting

If you choose to hand quilt some projects in this book, you will need a quilter's hoop to keep the fabric taut, as well as quilting needles called "betweens." To start, cut a thread about 18" long. Thread a needle, and knot the other end. Insert the needle just under the quilt top about 1" away from the point where you would like to begin quilting. Bring the needle up through the fabric, and pull the thread so that the knot pops through the top layer of fabric and is secured underneath. Take three or four small, evenly spaced running stitches, being sure to go through all three layers of the quilt. When the thread is nearly gone, make a small knot close to the fabric and pop the knot under the fabric.

Binding

Some of the projects in this book call for binding. On the smaller projects, I generally use prepackaged bias binding, but for some projects you may want to make your own, as I did for the "Chinese Lap Quilt" on page 24 and the "Indian Lap Quilt" on page 89. Follow the directions included with these projects to make your own binding.

ARABIC TILES
PLACE MAT AND NAPKIN

The border panel of this place mat and the napkin's appliqué make use of an ancient ceramist's artwork. Originally from a seventeenth century Arabic monastery, these designs from enameled tileworks make the perfect border because the design, which repeats, can be extended indefinitely. I chose a mottled fabric in a solid color for the center of the place mat to suggest the old wall these tiles might still be embedded in. The finished place mat measures 14" x 19" and the napkins are 19" square.

Materials: for 1 place mat and 1 napkin

(42"-wide fabric unless otherwise noted)

NOTE: The artwork is from *Arabic Art in Color,* edited by Prisse d'Avennes and published by Dover Books (see "Sources" on page 96 of this book). I used the artwork on page 27 of the Dover book.

3 June Tailor printer fabric sheets

1 yd. of yellow fabric

14½" x 19½" piece of low-loft batting

Yellow quilting thread

Air-soluble marking pen

If preparing the artwork with a photocopy machine, paper to match the outer edges of the place mat border and napkin designs.

Glue stick

Prepare the Artwork

Refer to "Preparing Artwork" on page 5.

PREPARING THE ARTWORK WITH A COMPUTER, SCANNER, AND PRINTER

Place Mat

The top and bottom borders of the place mat are identical, and each is made of three pieces: the left, middle, and right. For the left and right border pieces, you will need four lengths of border art 3" x 6¼" and for the middle pieces you will need two lengths of border art 3" x 8", including ¼" seam allowances. Using the book mentioned in the Note at left, scan the border artwork into the computer; it doesn't need to be enlarged or reduced. Crop the artwork so the border pieces match up along the ¼" seam line. Position your repeating border segments carefully, so that when they are finished, each will bisect one of the green, six-petal flowers in the center of the border—so that together, whole flowers are made.

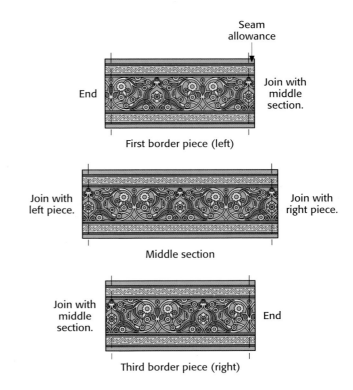

First border piece (left)

Middle section

Third border piece (right)

Create a bleed for the seam allowance around the border pieces (see "Printing" on page 7). If making the napkin, prepare the artwork for it as described below and print all the art out on 3 sheets of printer fabric to make maximum use of the sheets. Print the art onto the printer fabric; allow to dry. Rinse as suggested in "About the Printer Fabric" on page 5.

Napkin

The napkin design motif can be found on the same page of the artwork book as the border art. Reduce the image to 75 percent of the original size; create a bleed for a ⅛" seam allowance around the image. To save space, print this image onto the printer fabric sheets along with 2 shorter pieces of the place mat border; allow to dry. Rinse as suggested in "About the Printer Fabric" on page 5.

PREPARING ARTWORK WITH A PHOTOCOPIER

Using the book mentioned in the Note on page 13, have the artwork copied 6 times at full size and once at 75 percent. With a pair of scissors, cut out the border strips as indicated in "Preparing Artwork with a Computer, Scanner, and Printer" for the place mat above, omitting the reference to creating bleed. Paste the strips to a piece of colored paper that roughly matches the thin blue outer edges above and below the image. Cut out the napkin motif and place on a light colored background square of paper roughly matching the outer edge of the image. Cut around the images, leaving about ½" of colored paper around all edges. Arrange and glue the artwork to three pieces of white paper, using a glue stick. Copy on printer fabric sheets; allow to dry. Rinse as suggested in "About the Printer Fabric" on page 5.

Cutting

FOR THE PLACE MAT:

From the yellow fabric, cut:

  1 rectangle, 14½" x 19½" for the place mat back

  1 rectangle, 9½" x 19½" for the place mat center front panel

FOR THE NAPKIN:

From the yellow fabric, cut:

  1 square, 20" x 20"

From the printer fabric sheets, cut out the six border pieces to the measurements indicated in "Preparing the Artwork with a Computer, Scanner, and Printer." Cut out the napkin motif, allowing ⅛" all around for a turn-under allowance.

Making the Place Mat

1. Baste the border strips together along the seam allowances, using a fabric glue stick to ensure that the patterns line up properly; finger-press. Using the fold as a sewing guide, sew the border pieces right sides together; press the seam allowances open.

2. Pin the border strips to the long edges of the center front panel of the place mat; stitch ¼" from the raw edges. Press the seam allowances open.

3. Enlarge the quilting design on page 16 of this book 200 percent to fit the center panel of the place mat. Tape the pattern to a window or light box, then position the place mat top right side up over the photocopy so that the pattern is centered; tape in place. Trace the pattern design onto the fabric, using an air-soluble marking pen.

4. Place the place mat top, right side up over the batting; pin-baste every 3" to 4" (see "Layering and Basting" on page 10). Quilt on the marked lines, using free-motion quilting (see "Machine Quilting" on page 11).

5. Pin the place mat back over the place mat front, right sides together. Stitch ¼" from the raw edges, leaving a 9" opening on 1 of the short ends for turning the place mat right-side out. Trim the batting from the seam allowances; clip corners.

6. Turn the place mat right side out; slipstitch the opening closed.

Making the Napkin

1. Turn all edges of the napkin fabric under ¼"; press. Turn under ¼" again. Secure in place, if desired with a fabric glue stick. Machine-stitch close to the inside fold.

2. Fold under ⅛" around the edges of the napkin appliqué; press. Position the appliqué diagonally in 1 corner of the napkin; secure with a fabric glue stick. Stitch down by hand using small stitches.

Arabic Tiles Place Mat
Quilting Design

Enlarge pattern 200%.

ARCHITECTURAL COASTERS

I love traveling, and the pictures in the Dover book Illustrations of World-Famous Places *remind me why. You can make the coasters as shown here, or to commemorate a special trip, select illustrations of places you've been, through drawings, postcards, or even photos. Or you could choose fantasy places, places you've only dreamed of going! The finished coasters measure 4" x 4".*

Materials: for 4 coasters
(42"-wide fabric unless otherwise noted)

NOTE: The artwork for these coasters is from *Illustrations of World-Famous Places* by Charles Hogarth, published by Dover Books (see "Sources" on page 96 of this book).

2 June Tailor printer fabric sheets
¼ yd. fabric for backing or 4 scraps, each at least 4½" square (I used muslin)
16" x 16" piece of low-loft batting
Silver metallic quilting thread
Glue stick

Prepare the Artwork

NOTE: Refer to "Preparing Artwork" on page 5.

PREPARING ARTWORK WITH A COMPUTER, SCANNER, AND PRINTER

Scan in the lettering and quilting pattern for each coaster (pages 19 and 20 of this book) and the desired artwork. I used artwork from *Illustrations of World-Famous Places* (see Note above): on page 15 (Westminster Abbey, London); page 24 (Colosseum, Italy); page 30 (Taj Mahal, India); and page 32 (Osaka Castle, Japan). Crop the artwork closely on all sides, then change the document size to be 3½" tall. Copy this entire image and paste it into the file with the type and quilting pattern, positioning it within the center panel. Then, print out the image on a piece of colored paper and cut ¼" from the outermost border. For Japan, I used green; for Italy, pink; for England, blue; and for India, yellow. Select shades that are not too dark so that the images won't be obscured. The paper should also not be too textured or varied. Tape 2 of the coaster designs on 1 piece of white paper and scan them in. Then print out this file on a piece of printer fabric; allow to dry. Repeat for the other 2 designs. Rinse as suggested in "About the Printer Fabric" on page 5. You may also color the background using your image manipulation software and eliminate the need to re-scan your images.

PREPARING ARTWORK WITH A PHOTOCOPIER

Using art from the book mentioned in the Note at left, reduce it to fit within a 3¾" wide x 2½" tall area using a photocopy machine. Copy onto white paper. Also photocopy the typeface and quilting pattern for each coaster (pages 19 and 20 of this book) on white paper. Cut out the art and apply a light coat of glue to the back, using a glue stick; position the art within the center panel of the quilting pattern. Smooth out the paper, making sure there are no lumps of glue or creases. Have the images copied onto colored paper. For Japan, I used green; for Italy, pink; for England, blue; and for India, yellow. Select shades that are not too dark so that the images won't be obscured. The paper should not be too textured or varied. Cut out the images ¼" from the outermost border, and glue two per page on white paper. Copy each page onto a printer fabric sheet; allow to dry. Rinse as suggested in "About the Printer Fabric" on page 5.

Tip: If you choose to use images other than the ones I selected, set your type by using a word processing application or image-editing software, and use the lettering and quilting patterns on pages 19 and 20 as a guide.

Cutting

From the backing fabric, cut:
    4 squares, 4½" x 4½"

From the batting, cut:
    4 squares, 4" x 4"

From the printer fabric sheets, cut:
    4 coaster tops, 4½" square, centering
        an image in each square

Making the Coasters

1. Baste the batting squares to the wrong sides of the coaster tops, using a glue stick. Machine-quilt (see "Machine Quilting" on page 11) along the dotted lines using silver quilting thread.
2. Pin the coaster back to the coaster front, right sides together. Stitch ¼" from the raw edge of the coaster top, along the edge of the batting; leave a 3" opening on one side for turning the coasters right-side out. Trim the seam allowances.
3. Turn the coasters right side out and slipstitch the opening closed.

TAJ MAHAL

INDIA

OSAKA CASTLE

JAPAN

C O L O S S E U M

I T A L Y

W E S T M I N S T E R   A B B E Y

E N G L A N D

BUTTERFLY PILLOW

The butterflies on this patchwork pillow can be any size you want and can be arranged any way you like to create a variety of effects. The source for these images (see page 22) has many different butterflies to choose from, making it easy to customize the colors to your home. The finished pillow measures 16" x 16".

Materials

(42"-wide fabric unless otherwise noted)

NOTE: The butterfly images are from *Old-Time Butterfly Vignettes in Full Color,* selected and arranged by Carol Belanger Grafton, and published by Dover Books (see "Sources" on page 96 of this book).

> 5 June Tailor printer fabric sheets
> ⅝ yd. green fabric
> 16" x 16" pillow form
> 16½" x 16½" square of low-loft batting
> Green quilting thread (I used variegated Sulky thread to match the variations in the fabric.)
> If using a computer, 1 sheet blue textured paper, 8½" x 11"; if using a photocopy machine, 3 sheets blue textured paper, 8½" x 11"
> Air-soluble marking pen
> Ruler
> Glue stick

Prepare the Artwork

NOTE: Refer to "Preparing Artwork" on page 5.

PREPARING ARTWORK WITH A COMPUTER, SCANNER, AND PRINTER

Create a background pattern by scanning a piece of blue textured paper. Copy this background and paste it into a new file for each butterfly panel. Or, you can fill the files with a solid color using your computer. Use the following dimensions for your panels: 1 center panel, 6½" square; 4 corner panels 5½" square. Next, scan in the desired butterfly images. I used artwork from the book mentioned in the Note above: on plate 2, #21 and #34; plate 6, #92; plate 13, #195. Crop each butterfly closely and size the whole file to fit within the panels, allowing ¼" seam allowances all around. Vary the sizes of the butterflies and fit more than 1 in some of the panels. When you are happy with the sizes, select the butterfly only, then copy and paste it into a file with a background. See "Image-Editing Software" on page 6 for a discussion on how to select certain areas of an image file. Print each butterfly panel onto a printer fabric sheet; allow to dry. Rinse as suggested in "About the Printer Fabric" on page 5.

PREPARING ARTWORK WITH A PHOTOCOPIER

Cut the textured blue paper for the background of the panels into pieces with the following dimensions: 1 center panel, 6½" square; 4 corner panels 5½" square. Next, reduce or enlarge your butterflies to size on a black and white photocopier. I used artwork from the book mentioned in the Note at left: on plate 2, #21 and #34; plate 6, #92; plate 13, #195. When you are satisfied with the sizes, have them color copied. Cut out the art and apply a light coat of glue to the back, using a glue stick; position the images within the blue paper panels. Smooth out the art, making sure there are no lumps of glue or creases in the paper. Copy each panel onto a printer fabric sheet; allow to dry. Rinse as suggested in "About the Printer Fabric" on page 5.

Cutting

From the green fabric, cut:

4 pieces, 5½" x 6½" for the pieced pillow front

1 piece, 16½" x 16½" for the pillow back

From the printer fabric sheets, cut:

1 center panel, 6½" square

4 corner panels, 5½" square

Making the Pillow

1. Stitch the pillow panels into 3 horizontal rows of 3 panels each. Use a 5½" butterfly square for the first and last panel of the top and bottom rows; use a 5½" x 6½" piece of green fabric for the middle panels of the top and bottom rows. Use a 5½" x 6½" piece of green fabric for the first and last panel of the middle row; use a 6½" x 6½" butterfly square for the middle panel of the middle row.

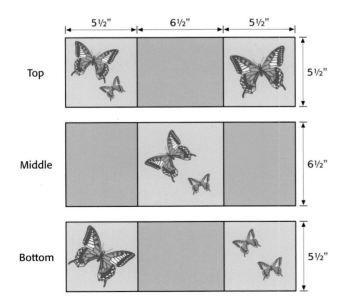

Stitch the three rows together to make the pillow top.

2. Pin the pillow top, right side up over the batting; pin-baste, spacing pins 3" to 4" apart (see "Layering and Basting" on page 10). Quilt in-the-ditch (see "Machine Quilting" on page 11) around each panel with green thread. Mark 5 diagonal lines, spaced 1" apart, in each of the green panels, using an air-soluble marking pen and a ruler, as shown below. Quilt on the marked lines.

3. Pin the pillow back to the pillow front, right sides together. Stitch ¼" from the edges of the pillow top, leaving a 12" opening for turning. Clip the corners and trim the seam allowances.

4. Turn the pillow cover right side out. Insert the pillow form; slipstitch the opening closed.

CHINESE LAP QUILT

This cozy lap quilt features nature-themed, intricately beautiful Chinese art. The square, uniform size of the different art pieces made them easy to work with and inspired me to use them like tiles. The finished lap quilt measures 54" x 62".

Materials

(42"-wide fabric unless otherwise noted)

Note: The artwork used in this lap quilt is from *Chinese Patterns,* part of the Shambhala Agile Rabbit Editions series, published by Shambhala Publications, Inc. (see "Sources" on page 96 of this book). I used the artwork on pages 103, 106, and 107 of the Shambhala book. The artwork in the Agile Rabbit Edition is also supplied on CD-ROM, in a variety of formats, which eliminates the need for scanning.

21 June Tailor printer fabric sheets
2 yds. for border, sashing strips,
 and binding
1⅞ yds. for inner border sashing strips
½ yd. for the Deer block
⅜ yd. for the Flower block
½ yd. for the Knotwork block
1¾ yds. 90"-wide muslin for backing
58" x 66" piece of low-loft batting
Invisible quilting thread
If preparing artwork with a photocopy
 machine, colored paper to match the
 edges of the artwork
Glue stick

Prepare the Artwork

NOTE: Refer to "Preparing Artwork" on page 5.

PREPARING ARTWORK WITH A COMPUTER, SCANNER, AND PRINTER

Using images from *Chinese Patterns* (see Note above), either scan in the artwork from the book or retrieve it from the accompanying CD if you have a CD-ROM drive. Size each piece of art to be 4" square. Then create 3 new files that are 4½" square and color them to match the outer edges of the three pieces of art, either by scanning colored paper or filling the background with a color on your computer. Copy and paste the artwork into the 4½" files. Print 2 images on each printer fabric sheet when possible. You can print 2 on the same sheet by creating a new file 4½" wide by 9" high, copying the finished artwork, and pasting 2 images into the new file. Print 9 sheets of the Deer block; 7 sheets of the Knotwork block, and 5 sheets of the Flower block; allow to dry. Rinse as suggested in "About the Printer Fabric" on page 5.

PREPARING ARTWORK WITH A PHOTOCOPIER

Using the *Chinese Patterns* book (see Note at left), copy the images on pages 103, 106, and 107 on a color copier, reducing the images to 4". Copy each piece of art twice. Mount each image centered in a 4¼" square of colored paper that closely matches the edge of the artwork; secure with a glue stick. Then glue the 2 copies of the same image together on a piece of white paper. Copy 9 sets of Deer blocks, 7 sets of Knotwork blocks, and 5 sets of Flower blocks onto printer fabric sheets; allow to dry. Rinse as suggested in "About the Printer Fabric" on page 5.

Tip: If you do not want to use as much printer fabric as is required for this project, replace the artwork in the outer rows with one of the other fabrics used in the project. This way, you'll need only 10 sheets instead of 21.

Cutting

From the fabric for the outer border, sashing strips, and binding, cut:
 2 strips, 3" x 48½" for the outer border
 2 strips, 3" x 62½" for the outer border

3 strips, 2½" x 38½" for the sashing
16 strips, 2½" x 6½" for the sashing
2 strips, 1½" x 40½" for the sashing
2 strips, 1½" x 30½" for the sashing
2 strips, 3" x 62½" for the binding
2 strips, 3" x 54½" for the binding

From the fabric for the inner border sashing strips, cut:

8 strips, 1½" x 6½"
18 strips, 2½" x 6½"
4 strips, 1½" x 56½"
4 strips, 1½" x 32½"

From the fabric for the Deer block, cut:

36 strips, 1½" x 6½"
36 strips, 1½" x 4½"

From the fabric for the Flower block, cut:

20 strips, 1½" x 6½"
20 strips, 1½" x 4½"

From the fabric for the Knotwork block, cut:

28 strips, 1½" x 6½"
28 strips, 1½" x 4½"

From the printer fabric sheets, cut:

18 Deer blocks, 10 Flower blocks, and 14 Knotwork blocks, each 4½" square

From the muslin, cut:

1 rectangle, 58" x 66" for the backing

Block Assembly

Assemble 18 Deer blocks, 10 Flower blocks, and 14 Knotwork blocks as shown. To make a Deer block, sew a 1½" x 4½" strip to the left and right side of a deer square. Then sew a 1½" x 6½" strip to the top and bottom of the deer square. Position the central image consistently. Repeat to make the Flower blocks, and the Knotwork blocks.

Quilt Assembly

1. Make the top and bottom pieced inner borders by arranging the blocks and sashing strips as shown below. You will need 2 Knotwork blocks, 5 Deer blocks, 2 of the 1½" x 6½" strips for the inner border sashing, 6 of the 2½" x 6½" strips for the inner border sashing, and 2 of the 1½" x 56½" strips for the inner border sashing, for each border.

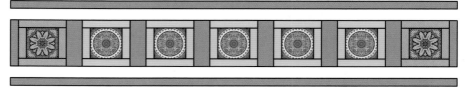

Make 2.

2. Make the pieced inner side borders by arranging the blocks and sashing strips as shown below. You will need 4 Deer blocks, 2 of the 1½" x 6½" strips for the inner border sashing, 3 of the 2½" x 6½" strips for the inner border sashing, and 2 of the 1½" x 32½" strips for the inner border sashing, for each side border.

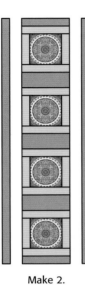

Make 2.

3. Make top and bottom rows of the quilt center by arranging the blocks and sashing strips as shown below. You will need 2 Knotwork blocks, 3 Flower blocks, and 4 of the 2½" x 6½" sashing strips, for each row.

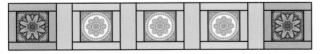

Make 2.

4. Make the middle 2 rows of the quilt center by arranging the blocks and sashing strips as shown below. You will need 3 Knotwork blocks, 2 Flower blocks, and 4 of the 2½" x 6½" sashing strips, for each row.

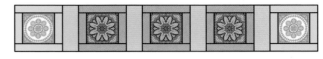

Make 2.

5. Assemble the center quilt panel as shown below using the 2½" x 38½" sashing strips between the rows. Then, sew the 1½" x 30½" sashing strips to the left and right sides of the quilt center. Sew the 1½" x 40½" sashing strips to the top and bottom.

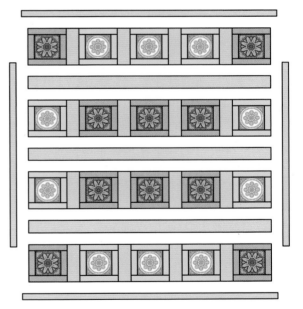

6. Sew the left and right pieced inner borders to the side edges of the center quilt panel as shown. Then sew the top and bottom pieced inner borders to the top and bottom edges of the center quilt panel.

7. Sew the 3" x 48½" outer border strips to the side edges of the quilt. Sew the 3" x 62½" outer border strips to the top and bottom edges of the quilt.

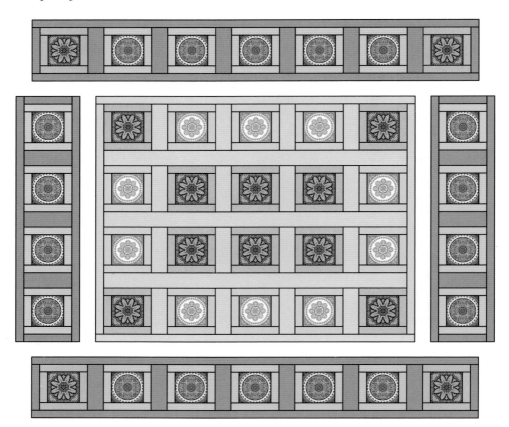

Finishing the Quilt

1. Layer the batting and backing with the quilt top; the batting and backing should extend 2" beyond the edges of the quilt top. Pin-baste the layers together every 3" to 4" (see "Layering and Basting" on page 10).

2. Quilt in-the-ditch on all sashing strips, using invisible thread (see "Machine Quilting" on page 11). Divide all 2" finished sashing strips the long way, by quilting a straight line down the middle of each. Trim the batting and backing even with the edges of the quilt top.

3. Fold the binding strips in half lengthwise, wrong sides together. Open the strips and press the raw edges ¼" to the wrong side. Refold the strips. Pin the shorter binding strips to the side edge of the quilt top, encasing the raw edges. Machine-stitch close to the inner fold, catching the binding on the back in the stitching. Trim any excess binding. Repeat with the top and bottom binding strips, turning in the raw edges at the ends.

FLORAL BOLSTER PILLOW

This pillow makes a comfortable neck rest and features flowers that bloom when summer is at its height. The illustrations, which were originally black and white, can be easily changed to mimic the uplifting hues of a flowering garden. The finished pillow measures 8" x 18".

Materials

(42"-wide fabric unless otherwise noted)

NOTE: Artwork is from *Ready-To-Use Floral Spot Illustrations*, by Stefen Bernath, published by Dover Books (see "Sources" on page 96 of this book). I used the daisies on page 10, the carnations on page 11, and the sunflower on page 14 of the Dover book.

> 2 June Tailor printer fabric sheets
> ½ yd. green leaf-print fabric
> 2 pieces of low-loft batting, each
>   8½" x 18½"
> Polyester fiberfill
> Off-white quilting thread
> If preparing artwork with a photocopy
>   machine, 2 sheets of off-white textured
>   paper, 8½" x 11"
> Air-soluble marking pen
> Glue stick

Prepare the Artwork

NOTE: Refer to "Preparing Artwork" on page 5.

PREPARING ARTWORK WITH A COMPUTER, SCANNER, AND PRINTER

Create 3 files, 4½" square. Create a background pattern by scanning a piece of off-white textured paper or fabric, or fill in the files with a solid color using your computer. Next, scan in the flower images listed in the Note above or choose your own. For each flower, do the following:

Crop the flower so the image fills most of the space. Choose a color on your computer for the flower, apply the color, then screen back the background color, making it several shades lighter. See "Image-Editing Software" on page 6 for different methods of coloring the background. I used muted shades of yellow for the sunflower, orange for the carnation, and purple

for the daisies. Size this file to be 3½" wide or tall; the image will be deformed if you try to make the image square.

Copy the file and paste it into one of the 4½" square files with the off-white background. Print 2 of the flowers on one printer fabric sheet and the remaining flower on a separate fabric sheet. You can print 2 images at a time by creating a new file 4½" wide by 9" high, copying the finished artwork, and pasting 2 images into the new file. Allow the printer fabric sheets to dry. Rinse as suggested in "About the Printer Fabric" on page 5.

PREPARING ARTWORK WITH A PHOTOCOPIER

Select off-white textured paper or fabric for the background of the art and cut 3 pieces of paper, each 4½" square. Next, use a black-and-white photocopy machine to copy the flower images listed in the Note at left (or select your own images), sizing them to fit in a 3½" square.

Tip: Cut a 3½"-square opening from the center of a piece of card stock, to use for visually "cropping" images so you can choose which parts you like.

Once you have determined the percentage at which the art needs to be copied, have all three flowers color-copied at this size. Color copiers are capable of changing the colors on an original document. So, when you take your black and white images to the photocopy center to be copied, bring a sample of the colors you would like the flowers and the backgrounds to be. I used muted shades of yellow for the sunflower, orange for the carnation, and purple for the daisies. Have the art copied onto colored paper that is a few shades lighter than the flower colors.

Cut out the colored images to 3½" square and mount them centered within the off-white backgrounds using a glue stick. Then mount the flowers on two pieces of white paper. Smooth out the art, making sure there are no lumps of glue or creases in the paper. Copy each page onto a printer fabric sheet; allow to dry. Rinse as suggested in "About the Printer Fabric" on page 5.

Cutting

From the green leaf-print, cut:
 2 strips, 1½" x 4½" for the sashing
 2 strips, 2½" x 18½" for the top and bottom borders
 2 strips, 2½" x 8½" for the side borders
 1 piece, 8½" x 18½" for the backing

From the printer fabric sheets, cut:
 3 flower blocks, centering each image inside a 4½" square

Making the Pillow

1. Piece the flowers and 1½" x 4½" sashing strips together in the order shown below.
2. Pin the top and bottom border strips to the long edges of the pieced unit, centering the border on the pieced unit. The border should extend 2½" at each end. Stitch the borders in place, starting and stopping ¼" from the corners of the pieced unit. Repeat with the side border strips. The ends of the border strips will overlap.

3. Pin the outer edges of adjacent border strips right sides together; the flower panel at the corner you are working on will have to be folded diagonally. Mark a 45-degree line extending from the corner of the flower panel to the outer edges of the border strips, using an air-soluble marking pen; sew along the marked line. Trim ¼" from the seam; press the seam allowances open.

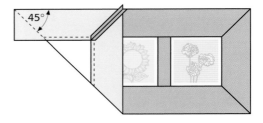

4. Layer the pillow top right side up over 1 of the 8½" x 18½" pieces of batting; baste (see "Layering and Basting" on page 10). Quilt in the ditch on all seams with off-white quilting thread (see "Machine Quilting" on page 11).
5. Machine-baste the backing fabric to the remaining piece of 8½" x 18½" batting, stitching ¼" from the edges. With right sides together, stitch the pillow top to the back, leaving a 6" opening on 1 short side for turning right side out. Clip the corners and trim any excess batting from the seams.
6. Turn the pillow right side out and stuff with polyester fiberfill. Slipstitch the opening closed.

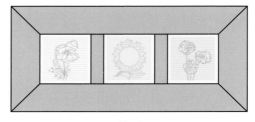

Quilt Plan

SHELL WALL HANGING

This quilted wall hanging has the feel of a framed print. I chose some beautiful shell illustrations and a hand-dyed blue solid fabric reminiscent of water for a summertime look. The book I found these illustrations in has over a thousand pictures of birds, insects, fish, and many other animals, allowing you to customize your "framed print" to fit your personality. The finished wall hanging measures 8" x 18".

Materials

(42"-wide fabric unless otherwise noted)

NOTE: The images used in this wall hanging were taken from *Animals: 1419 Copyright-Free Illustrations of Mammals, Birds, Fish, Insects, etc; A Pictorial Archive from Nineteenth-Century Sources*, selected by Jim Harter, published by Dover Books (see "Sources" on page 96 of this book). The shells I used are on pages 272–273 of the Dover book (#1371, #1383, and #1385).

> 2 June Tailor printer fabric sheets
> ½ yd. mottled blue fabric (I used Bali hand-dyed solids by Hoffman)
> 1 piece of low-loft batting, 8" x 18"
> Blue quilting thread
> Prepackaged off-white double-fold bias binding, ⅞" wide
> Wood dowel, ⅛" diameter
> If preparing the artwork with a photocopy machine, 2 sheets of textured, sand-colored paper
> Glue stick

Prepare the Artwork

NOTE: Refer to "Preparing Artwork" on page 5.

PREPARING ARTWORK WITH A COMPUTER, SCANNER, AND PRINTER

Create files, 4½" square. Create a background pattern by scanning a piece of textured, sand-colored paper or fabric, or fill the files with a solid color using your computer; see "Image-Editing Software" on page 6. Next, scan in the shell images listed in the Note above or choose your own.

Rotate the shell images so they are positioned as desired. Choose different colors on your computer for each shell; I used earth tones.

Crop the images as close as possible on the left and right sides. Size the scallop and the solarium to be 2½" wide, and size the volute to be 3" tall.

Select and copy the shells, and paste them into the 4½" square background files. Type in the shell identification centered about ½" beneath each shell. I used 24 point Times Roman italic. Print 2 shell images on 1 printer fabric sheet and print the other on a separate printer fabric sheet. You can print 2 on the same sheet by creating a new file 4½" wide by 9" high, copying the finished artwork, and pasting 2 images into the new file. Allow the printed fabric to dry. Rinse as suggested in "About the Printer Fabric" on page 5.

Tip: If your image-editing software doesn't allow you to incorporate a typeface, set the type separately, using a word processing application as described below in "Preparing Artwork with a Photocopier".

PREPARING ARTWORK WITH A PHOTOCOPIER

Copy the shell artwork listed in the Note at left onto white paper using a black-and-white photocopy machine (or choose your own images); size the scallop and the solarium to be 2½" wide, and size the volute to be 3" tall. Set the shell identification lettering on a word-processing application, or use press type, stencils, or calligraphy to spell out the shell names. Glue 2 of the shell images and lettering to a piece of white paper and the other shell and lettering to its own piece of paper, properly sized and arranged as desired. Smooth out the art, making sure there are no lumps of glue or creases in the paper. Since the original is black and white, bring a sample of the colors you would like the shells to be to the copy center (I used earth tones). Have the shells colored and copied onto the sand-colored paper you've selected for the background. Copy each page onto a printer fabric sheet;

allow to dry. Rinse as suggested in "About the Printer Fabric" on page 5.

Cutting

From the mottled blue fabric, cut:
  2 strips, 1½" x 4½" for the sashing
  2 strips, 2¼" x 18½" for the side borders
  2 strips, 2¼" x 8½" for the top and bottom borders
  1 piece, 8" x 18" for the backing

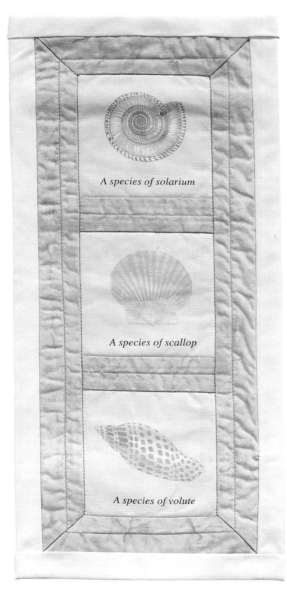

From the printer fabric sheets, cut:
  3 shell images with type, each 4½" square, positioning the images within the squares as desired

Making the Wall Hanging

1. Piece the shells and 1½" x 4½" sashing strips together as shown.

2. Center the side border strips on the side edges of the pieced unit; pin. The border will extend 2½" at each end. Stitch the borders in place, starting and stopping ¼" from the corners of the pieced unit. Repeat with the top and bottom border strips. The ends of the border strips will overlap.

3. Bring the outer edges of the border strips right sides together and pin in place; the shell panel adjacent to the corner you are working on will have to be folded diagonally. Mark a 45-degree angle extending

from the corner of the flower panel to the outer edge of the border, and sew along this line. Trim ¼" from the seam; then press the seam allowances open.

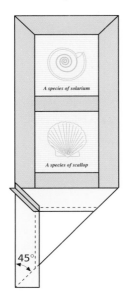

4. Place the backing fabric wrong side up; layer with batting. Place the quilt top right side up over the batting; baste (see "Layering and Basting" on page 10). Quilt in the ditch on all seams with blue quilting thread and across the middle of the 2 sashing strips (see "Machine Quilting" on page 11). Also quilt ½" from the inner edges of the border panels all around.

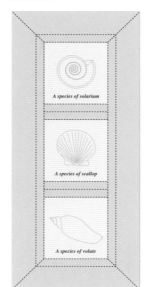

5. Cut 2 pieces of binding 18½" long. Unfold the binding; pin right sides together to the left and right front sides of the wall hanging. Stitch along the first fold line. Turn the binding to the back; press. Slipstitch in place; trim excess at ends. Cut 2 pieces of binding 9" long; stitch to the top and bottom of the wall hanging as for the sides, allowing ½" to extend at each end. Turn in the excess fabric at the ends. Slipstitch in place on the back side and along the ends.

6. Cut a piece of binding 6" long. Turn the raw edges ¼" to the wrong side at the ends; secure with fabric glue. Hand stitch the binding to the back of the quilt along the long edges 2½" down from the upper edge of the quilt. Cut the dowel to 7½" long. Insert the dowel into the binding sleeve for hanging. To hang, rest the dowel on 2 small nails or cup hooks.

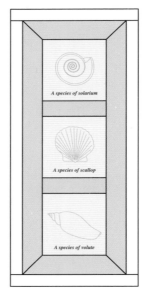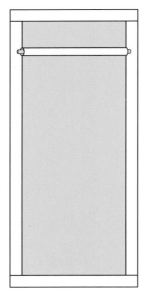

Quilt Plan

SOOTHING SLEEP SACHETS

This pair of sachets can be hung from the doorknob of a guest room or kept near your own bed. Stuffed with a customized recipe of relaxing fragrant herbs, it's a pleasant accent to any bedroom. The star sachet measures 6" tall and the moon sachet measures 6½" tall.

good night
bonne nuit
buoa notte
buena noche

dreams
rêves
sogni
sueños

Materials

(42"-wide fabric unless otherwise noted)

NOTE: The artwork for this project is by Biz Stone and can be found on pages 40–43.

> 4 June Tailor printer fabric sheets
> 4 pieces low-loft batting, 8½" square
> Silver metallic quilting thread
> 37" length of silver cord
> Air-soluble marking pen
> Point turner
> Glue stick
> 2 cups "Soothing Sleep Sachet Mix" (see recipe on page 39)

Prepare the Artwork

NOTE: Refer to "Preparing Artwork" on page 5.

PREPARING ARTWORK WITH A COMPUTER, SCANNER, AND PRINTER

Scan the front and back images for each sachet (pages 40–43 in this book) at 100 percent. Print 1 image per sheet of printer fabric; allow to dry. Rinse as suggested in "About the Printer Fabric" on page 5.

PREPARING THE ARTWORK WITH A PHOTOCOPIER

Copy the front and back images for each sachet (pages 40–43 in this book) at 100 percent, using 1 sheet of printer fabric for each image; allow to dry. Rinse as suggested in "About the Printer Fabric" on page 5.

Making the Sachets

1. Baste a piece of batting to the back of each fabric image by using a glue stick, making sure that the entire image is backed. On each piece of fabric, machine-quilt a border ⅛" inside the edge of the image all around using silver quilting thread. Also quilt lines coming from some of the stars as indicated in the illustrations below.

Quilt the same border and some of the stars in a similar manner on the back of the sachets.

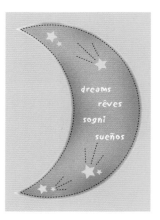

2. Trim the quilted pieces ¼" from the outer edges of the designs.
3. Cut an 18½" piece of cord for each sachet. Glue the ends of 1 piece to the top point of the star front on the right side, within the seam allowance; glue the ends of the

second piece 2½" from the top point of the moon front, on the outer curve, in the same manner.

4. Pin the front and back sachet pieces right sides together. Sew ¼" from the raw edges of the fabric. To leave enough room for turning the sachets right side out and, stuffing them, stop at the two bottom points of the star and leave a 3" opening on the moon's outer curve.

5. Trim the seam allowances to ⅛" and clip almost to the stitching line on the 4 inside corners of the star and all around the moon, to prevent puckering.

6. Turn the sachets right side out and use a point turner to gently push out the points. Make a knot at the base of the cord, if desired.

7. Make the "Soothing Sleep Sachet Mix." Stuff each sachet with 1 cup of the sachet mix and slipstitch the opening closed.

"Soothing Sleep Sachet Mix"

by Mandy Stone, herbal scholar

Makes 2 cups.
In a bowl, mix together:
   ½ cup mugwort, to help remember dreams
   ½ cup lavender, to ease headaches and reduce stress
   ½ cup sweet hops, for relaxation
   ¼ cup German chamomile flowers, for calmness and pleasant dreams
   ¼ cup rose petals, for peacefulness

good night
bonne nuit
buoa notte
buena noche

Star Front

Star Back

Moon Front

Moon Back

MAIL HOLDER

This convenient pocketed wall hanging features vintage stamps from all over the world, adding a little international flavor to daily life. The finished mail holder measures 12" x 16".

Materials

(42"-wide fabric unless otherwise noted)

NOTE: The artwork for this project is by Biz Stone and can be found on pages 48 and 49.

> 2 June Tailor printer fabric sheets
> ½ yd. yellow fabric
> ⅜ yd. muslin for backing
> ½ yd. low-loft batting
> 12" x 16" piece of matboard or thin, non-corrugated cardboard
> Off-white and yellow quilting thread and invisible thread
> 1 package off-white double fold bias binding, ¼" wide
> 1 package taupe binding, ½" wide
> ½ yd. cord for hanging
> Air-soluble marking pen
> Permanent fabric glue
> Spray adhesive
> Glue stick

Prepare the Artwork

NOTE: Refer to "Preparing Artwork" on page 5.

PREPARING ARTWORK WITH A COMPUTER, SCANNER, AND PRINTER

Scan "mail," "stamps," "pens & pencils," and the envelope art on pages 48 and 49. Fit all the images on 2 sheets of printer fabric and print; allow to dry. Rinse as suggested in "About the Printer Fabric" on page 5.

PREPARING ARTWORK WITH A PHOTOCOPIER

Copy "mail," "stamps," "pens & pencils," and the envelope art from pages 48 and 49 onto 2 sheets of printer fabric; dry and rinse as suggested in "About the Printer Fabric" on page 5.

Cutting

From the batting, cut:
> 1 rectangle, 11½" x 15½" for the front of the mail holder
> 1 rectangle, 2½" x 11½" for the narrow top pocket
> 1 rectangle, 5¾" x 11½" for the large bottom pocket
> 1 rectangle, 4" x 8" for the "envelope" pocket.

From the yellow fabric, cut:
> 1 rectangle, 12" x 16" for the front of the mail holder
> 2 rectangles, 2½" x 12" for the narrow pocket
> 2 rectangles, 6" x 12" for the large pocket.

From the muslin, cut:
> 1 rectangle, 12" x 16" for the backing
> 1 rectangle, 4½" x 8½" for the envelope pocket

From the printer fabric sheets, cut:
> The envelope art along the colored edge
> 3 labels, ¼" from the red borders

Making the Mail Holder

1. Center and baste the 2½" x 11½" piece of batting to the wrong side of one of the 2½" x 12" rectangles of yellow fabric, using a glue stick; ¼" of fabric should extend past the batting on both short ends.

2. Prepare the "mail," "stamps," "pens & pencils" labels by folding the corners under diagonally and then turning the ¼" seam allowances to the back; secure with dabs of glue. Allow a thin area of white around the red outlines.

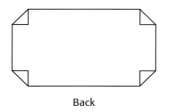

Back

3. Position both labels on the fabric backed with batting. The labels should both be ⅞" down from the upper edge of the yellow fabric; the "stamps" label should be 1⅜" in from the left edge of the yellow fabric, and the "pens" label should be 2⅛" in from the right edge. This will center the labels within their pockets after all the binding is applied and the pockets are stitched down. Glue-baste the labels in place. Stitch the labels into position along the red border using invisible thread to create a perforated look.

4. Quilt a ¼" border all around the labels with yellow thread. Glue-baste the remaining piece of 2½" x 12" yellow fabric to the back of the labeled fabric.

5. Cut a 12" strip of ¼" binding. Enclose the raw upper edges of the labeled pocket with binding; edgestitch along the inside fold, using invisible thread.

6. To make the envelope pocket, center and glue-baste the 4" x 8" rectangle of batting to the wrong side of envelope art, right sides up. Place the 4½" x 8½" rectangle of muslin over the envelope art, right sides together; pin. Stitch the layers together ¼" from the edge, leaving a 3" opening on one of the short sides for turning. Clip the corners. Turn the pocket right side out; slipstitch the opening closed.

7. Pin 1 of the 6" x 12" rectangles of yellow fabric to the 5¾" x 11½" piece of batting, with ¼" of the fabric extending past the batting on the left, right, and bottom sides. Cut another 12" strip of off-white ¼" binding and stitch to the top of the rectangle as in step 5.

8. Place the envelope pocket on the 6" x 12" pocket, ⅞" below the binding strip, centered horizontally. Stitch the envelope pocket in place ⅛" from the edges of the envelope, leaving the upper edge open; use off-white thread.

9. Center and glue-baste the 11½" x 15½" piece of batting to the wrong side of the 12" x 16" rectangle of yellow fabric. The fabric should extend ¼" beyond the batting on all sides. Prepare the mail label in the same way as for the other labels, following step 2. Baste it to the 12" x 16" rectangle, centered across the 12" width, 2" from the upper edge. Stitch it down with invisible thread, and quilt a border ¼" and ¾" from the edges of the label with yellow thread.

10. To attach the narrow pocket to the background, first cut another 12" strip of the ¼" binding and use a little glue to attach it to the bottom of the pocket, encasing the raw edges. Pin the pocket to the background 2" from the lower edge of the mail label with

the side edges aligned, then stitch the 2 short side edges of the pocket to the background. Then stitch the pocket down $\frac{1}{16}$" from the edge of the binding strip using invisible thread. To separate the 2 pockets, use yellow thread to stitch between them vertically 1" from the right edge of the "stamps" label.

11. To attach the large pocket to the background, align the left, right, and bottom edges of the background and the large pocket; pin. Stitch down $\frac{1}{4}$" from these edges. Cut two 16" lengths of $\frac{1}{2}$" taupe binding. Unfold the binding; pin right sides together to the side edges of the mail holder. Stitch along the first fold line. Fold the binding flat to the right side. Cut two 13" lengths of binding for the top and bottom edges. Stitch the binding to the top and bottom of the mail holder in the same manner as for the sides, extending the binding $\frac{1}{2}$" beyond each side edge of the mail holder. Stop stitching at the sides when you reach the first fold in the side binding strips.

12. Attach the remaining muslin to the back of the matboard and the mail holder to the front of the matboard, using spray adhesive. Bring the side binding to the back. Insert 2" of cord within the fold of the binding on both sides, so that the cord emerges 2½" from the top of the mail holder. Then use permanent fabric glue to secure the cord and binding in place. Turn in the raw edges of the top and bottom binding at the sides. Fold binding to the back; secure with permanent fabric glue.

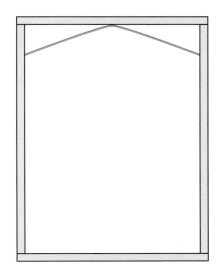

Quilt Plan

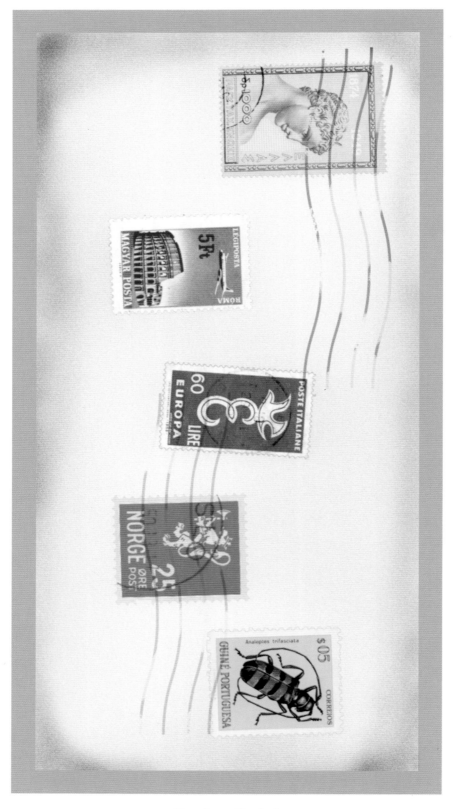

Envelope Pocket

mail

pens & pencils

stamps

Labels

QUILTED PICTURE FRAMES

These customized frames are perfect for a treasured picture. For added dimension, I accented the centers of the flowers on the smaller frame with silver beads. The small frame measures 6" x 8¾" and the large frame measures 7" x 10¾".

Materials: (for 2 frames)
(42"-wide fabric unless otherwise noted)

NOTE: Artwork for this project was taken from *Treasury of Illuminated Borders* in Full Color, edited by Carol Belanger Grafton, published by Dover Books (see "Sources" on page 96 of this book). I used the artwork on pages 1 and 47 of the Dover book.

3 June Tailor printer fabric sheets

¼ yd. muslin for backing

3 pieces low-loft batting, 8" x 10"

Off-white and silver metallic quilting thread

1 package off-white double-fold bias binding, ¼" wide, for the large frame

Silver paint marker (optional)

40 silver beads, 3mm

Matboard

Permanent fabric glue

Glue stick

Spray adhesive

If preparing artwork with a photocopy machine, colored paper to match the inner and outer edges of the frame image

Craft knife

16" length of ribbon for hanger on small frame

10" length of ribbon for hanger on large frame

8½" x 11" sheet of acetate

Prepare the Artwork

NOTE: Refer to "Preparing Artwork" on page 5.

PREPARING ARTWORK WITH A COMPUTER, SCANNER, AND PRINTER

To make the small frame, scan in the art on page 1 of *Treasury of Illuminated Borders in Full Color* (see Note at left) and size it to fit on the 8½" x 11" piece of printer fabric. The maximum size should be no more than 7½" x 10", though you should print out the frame first on paper to be sure your printer doesn't crop some of the image off. Add bleed to the outer and inner edges of the frame (see "Printing" on page 7). Print the frame on 1 printer fabric sheet.

To make the large frame, scan in the art on page 47 of the artwork book, and size it to be no more than 7½" wide; save the document. Add bleed to the outer and inner edges of the frame (see "Printing" on page 7); crop out the part of the image that hangs over the center opening. The frame will need to be made out of 2 pieces; to do this, crop out the bottom half of the image and save the document under another name. Open the original file again, and crop out the top half of the image. Save this document under another name as well. Print out the top and bottom halves on paper first to check whether they print out accurately, then print them on 2 printer fabric sheets; allow to dry. Rinse as suggested in "About the Printer Fabric" on page 5.

PREPARING ARTWORK WITH A PHOTOCOPIER

To make the frames, use artwork from *Treasury of Illuminated Borders in Full Color* (see Note at left). Cut strips of colored paper to fit around the inner and outer edges of the frames; use spray adhesive to attach the strips to the original or a photocopy (you could also leave the edges white). For the larger frame, make sure the paper strips cover the part of the image that hangs over the center opening so that the interior edges are straight. Have the frame on page 1 of the artwork book copied to fit on an 8½" x 11" sheet of printer fabric; test fit the image on paper first. Have the frame on page 47 of the artwork book copied to be about 7½" wide; this frame will need to have the top and bottom halves copied on separate printer fabric sheets; allow the printed fabric to dry. Rinse as suggested in "About the Printer Fabric" on page 5.

Making the Frames

1. Baste the 8" x 10" pieces of batting to the wrong sides of the printer fabric, using a glue stick. Quilt the frames as shown using silver thread for the small frame and off-white thread for the large frame (see "Machine Quilting" on page 11).

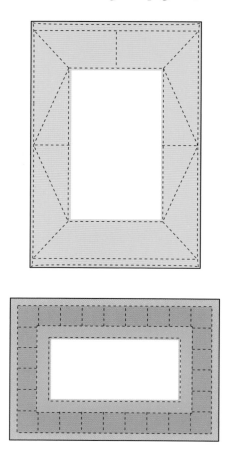

2. On the small frame sew a 3mm silver bead to the center of each flower around the border. After quilting and beading the frames, cut out the center opening, leaving ½" extra fabric all around for turning under. Snip the corners diagonally almost to the image.

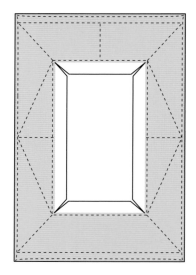

Fold the flaps to the wrong side; secure with permanent fabric glue.

3. Measure the frames; for each frame, cut out 2 pieces of matboard to the measured dimensions, plus 1 piece where the length and width is ¼" less (this piece of board will be the frame back). My small frame was 6¼" x 8¾" and the larger one was 7¼" x 10¾." For each frame, measure the center opening, as well as the distance of the inner edges to the outer edges of the frame, because the opening may not be exactly centered. Mark these measurements on 1 of the 2 boards that are the same size; cut out the opening. The quilted fabric frame will be mounted to this piece of board. Finally, cut out the interior opening on the second board, cutting the length and width ½" more than the actual frame opening. This board will be placed between the front and back boards, and will create a recessed area to hold pictures.

4. Before attaching the quilted fabric frames to the matboards with the smaller openings, I treated the interior edges of the boards so they would blend in with the fabric better. For the smaller frame, I used a silver paint marker to color the edges; for the larger frame, I glued a strip of prepackaged ¼" bias binding around each edge. After treating the edges, glue the board with the larger opening to the back of the board with the treated edges.

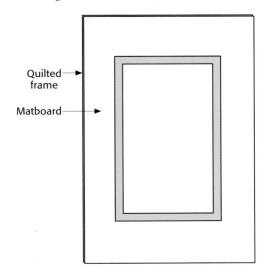

Quilted frame

Matboard

Then glue the quilted frame top to the side of the joined boards with the smaller interior opening.

5. To finish the outer edges of the small frame, I folded each corner under diagonally, glued it down, then folded the flaps over and glued them down. For the larger frame, I trimmed the edges of the quilted top even with the edges of the matboard and glued ¼" binding to the edges. To do this, cut 2 strips of binding the exact length of the frame, then glue them to the left and right sides, encasing the raw edges of the fabric and the edge of the mat board. Measure the width and cut 2 binding strips to this size plus ½"; glue these to the top and bottom of the frame, turning in the raw edges at the ends.

6. Cut a piece of muslin ½" larger than the frame back all around. Cut a second piece of muslin ⅛" smaller than the frame back all around. Attach the larger muslin piece to 1 side of the frame back with spray adhesive. Fold the corners under diagonally; secure with permanent fabric glue; fold the flaps over, securing with glue.

7. Secure each end of the ribbon hanger to the inside of the frame back with permanent fabric glue. Position the ends about 2" apart on the large frame and 5" apart on the small frame. Cover the inside of the frame back with the smaller piece of muslin, securing with spray adhesive.

8. Cut a piece of acetate ½" larger than the actual frame's opening and glue the edges to the recessed area of the frame opening. Glue the back of the frame on along the side and bottom edges. From the top of the frame, use tweezers to insert the photo in place.

VINE TABLE RUNNER

Real leaves and handmade paper were used to make the artwork for this table runner, so I chose coordinating fabrics in leafy hues and free-form quilting patterns to complete the natural theme. The finished runner measures 18" x 60".

Materials

(42"-wide fabric unless otherwise noted)

NOTE: The artwork is by Biz Stone and can be found on pages 58–60.

6 June Tailor printer fabric sheets
¼ yd. sage green for pieced center
¼ yd. medium green for pieced center
⅝ yd. brown vine print for border
⅝ yd. 90"-wide muslin for backing
20½" x 62½" piece of low-loft batting
Dark green quilting thread, and thread to match the vines in the border fabric

Prepare the Artwork

NOTE: Refer to "Preparing Artwork" on page 5

PREPARING ARTWORK WITH A COMPUTER, SCANNER, AND PRINTER

Scan the artwork on pages 58-60 at 100 percent. Create a 7½" wide x 9" tall file. Copy the single leaf image and paste it into the new document. Then flip the original scanned image horizontally or vertically, and copy and paste it into the document again. You will need to print this document twice on the printer fabric for a total of 4 pieces of art. Print each of the double leaf images 2 times, 1 to a page. Flip some of the images as described above; allow to dry. Rinse as suggested in "About the Printer Fabric" on page 5.

PREPARING ARTWORK WITH A PHOTOCOPIER

Copy the images on pages 58–60 at 100 percent, and have some of the images flipped horizontally or vertically. On 2 sheets of printer fabric, copy the single leaves, with 2 images on the page. Copy 4 of the double leaf images, each on their own page; flip some of these images horizontally or vertically as well. Allow the printer fabric sheets to dry. Rinse as suggested in "About the Printer Fabric" on page 5.

Cutting

From each of the sage green and the medium green fabrics, cut:
    6 rectangles, 4½" x 7½"
    2 rectangles, 6½" x 7½"

From the brown vine-print fabric, cut:
    6 rectangles, 3½" x 14½"
    4 rectangles, 3½" x 16½"

From the muslin, cut:
    1 rectangle, 20½" x 62½" for the backing

From the printer fabric sheets, cut:
    The single leaf images to measure
        4½" x 7½"
    The double leaf images to measure
        6½" x 7½"

Making the Table Runner

1. Stitch together 3 pieces of fabric for each of the 8 rows of the runner. Use 1 piece of each of the green fabrics and a piece of printer fabric. Vary the position of the fabrics in each row.

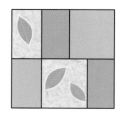

Row 1
Stitch each of the eight rows together following the Quilt Plan.

2. Stitch together the first and second rows to make section A, the third and fourth rows to make section B, the fifth and sixth rows to make section C, and the seventh and eighth rows to make section D.

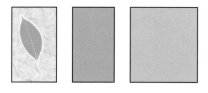

Rows 1 and 2
Stitch rows 3 and 4, 5 and 6, and 7 and 8 to each other in the same way.

3. To the top of section A and to the bottom of section D, sew a strip of the 3½" x 14½" brown fabric. Then, sew a 3½" x 16½" strip of brown fabric to the sides of both sections.

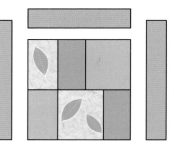

Section A

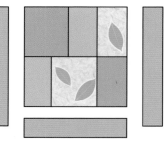

Section D

4. Sew the remaining 4 brown fabric strips measuring 4" x 14½" to the sides of sections B and C.

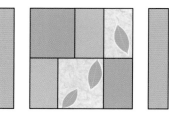

Section B

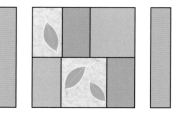

Section C

5. Stitch all the sections together.

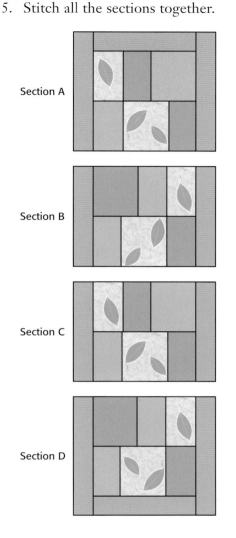

Section A

Section B

Section C

Section D

6. Layer the quilt top, batting, and backing; pin-baste as in "Layering and Basting" on page 10. Quilt around the edge of each leaf with dark green thread, and quilt a free-form vine across the runner connecting all the leaves (see "Machine Quilting" and "Hand Quilting" on page 11). In each of the green blocks, quilt a free-form vine pattern using thread to match the color of the vines in the border fabric. Start with a diagonal curved line going from 1 corner of each block to the opposite corner, then quilt offshoots from this main branch, then offshoots from the secondary branches.

7. Place the backing fabric over the runner top, right sides together. Stitch ¼" from the raw edges, leaving a 12" opening on one long side for turning. Trim across corners. Turn the runner right side out. Slipstitch the opening closed.

Quilt Plan

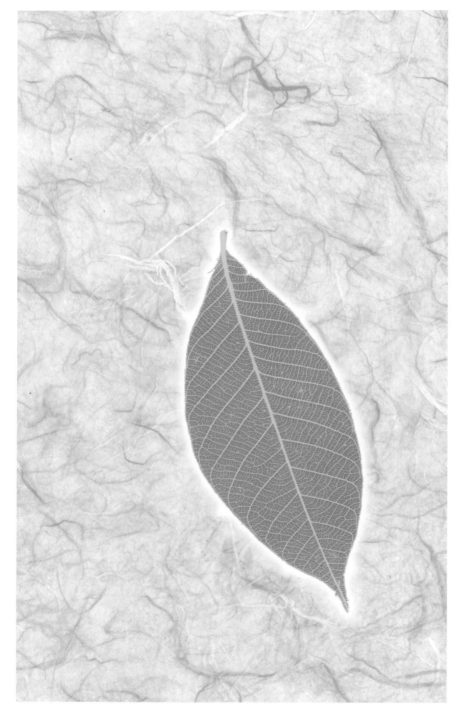

Single Leaf

Double Leaf 1

Double Leaf 2

WALL VASE

The design used on this wall vase is a detail from an illustration of a wrought-iron gate. Use the vase to display dried flowers from your garden, or fill it with dried herbs such as sage and lavender and hang it in your kitchen. The finished vase measures 8½" tall and 5½" across the top.

Materials

(42"-wide fabric unless otherwise noted)

NOTE: The artwork used in this wall vase was taken from *Ornamental Ironwork* by Eugene-Antoine Durenne, published by Dover Books (see "Sources" on page 96 of this book). The ironwork image I used is on page 114 of the Dover book, center bottom row.

> 2 June Tailor printer fabric sheets
> 2 pieces of muslin, at least 6" x 9", for the vase lining
> 2 pieces of low-loft batting, 6" x 9"
> Green quilting thread
> 6" length of ribbon, ¼" wide
> Air-soluble marking pen
> Permanent fabric glue
> Glue stick
> If preparing artwork with a photocopy machine, 2 sheets of green paper, 8½" x 11"
> 6 mother-of-pearl beads, 4mm
> 2 mother-of-pearl beads, 3mm

Prepare the Artwork

NOTE: Refer to "Preparing Artwork" on page 5.

PREPARING THE ARTWORK WITH A COMPUTER, SCANNER, AND PRINTER

Create a 6" wide x 9" tall file, and fill the document with a solid color using your computer (see "Image-Editing Software" on page 6). Then, scan the artwork listed in the Note above (or choose your own) and size it to be 6½" tall. Select and copy the image, then paste it onto the colored background. Fill any small white spaces within the image by selecting the area and filling it with the background color. You could also print the properly sized image on a piece of visually interesting paper, then scan the image again. (But beware—if you simply copied and pasted the image onto this kind of background, you wouldn't be able to match the white spaces in the image to your background pattern very easily.) Print out the image twice on the printer fabric; allow to dry. Rinse as suggested in "About the Printer Fabric" on page 5.

PREPARING THE ARTWORK WITH A PHOTOCOPIER

Copy the artwork listed in the Note at left (or choose your own) onto a piece of green paper; size the image to be 6½" tall. Copy the colored image once onto each of the 2 printer fabric sheets; allow to dry. Rinse as suggested in "About the Printer Fabric" on page 5.

Making the Wall Vase

1. Trace or photocopy the vase pattern (page 64) onto paper. Cut around the outer marked line. Center the vase pattern over the design on the printer fabric. Trace around the outer edge of the pattern, using an air-soluble marking pen. Repeat with the second image.

2. Baste a piece of batting to the wrong side of the printer fabric, using a glue stick; be sure that the entire image is backed. Repeat for the second image. Mark quilting lines ⅛" from the ironwork images with an air-soluble marking pen.

3. Machine-quilt around the images on the marked lines, using free-motion quilting (see "Machine Quilting" on page 11). On 1 piece, sew a 4mm bead on each of the 6 round knobs at the end of each branch of the image; sew the 3mm beads to the knobs closest to the main stem of the image.

4. Cut out the vase pieces along the outer marked pattern line. Pin the 2 pieces right sides together. Starting ¼" from the edge at the top, stitch all the way around, stopping ¼" from the top on the other side; backstitch at both ends.

5. Trim the seam allowances to ⅛" and trim away the excess batting; at the top, trim the batting ¼" from the edges. Turn the vase right-side out.

6. Form a loop with the 6" ribbon; align the ends. Attach the ribbon 1¾" from the top of the unbeaded side of the wall vase, on the inside, using permanent fabric glue.

7. Cut 2 vase lining pieces from the muslin, using the vase lining pattern on page 65. Sew them together as in steps 4 and 5, omitting the reference to the batting. Finger-press the top of the lining down ¼" to the wrong side. Fold the edges of the vase ¼" to the inside, then insert the lining into the vase. Align and pin the vase and lining together around the upper edges; slipstitch in place. Topstitch ¼" from the upper edge of the vase.

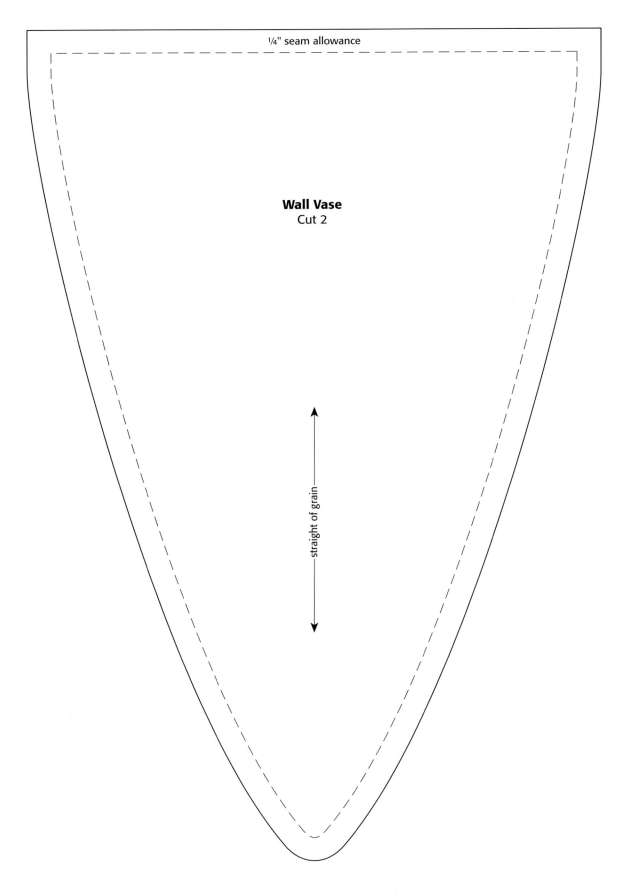

¼" seam allowance

Wall Vase
Cut 2

straight of grain

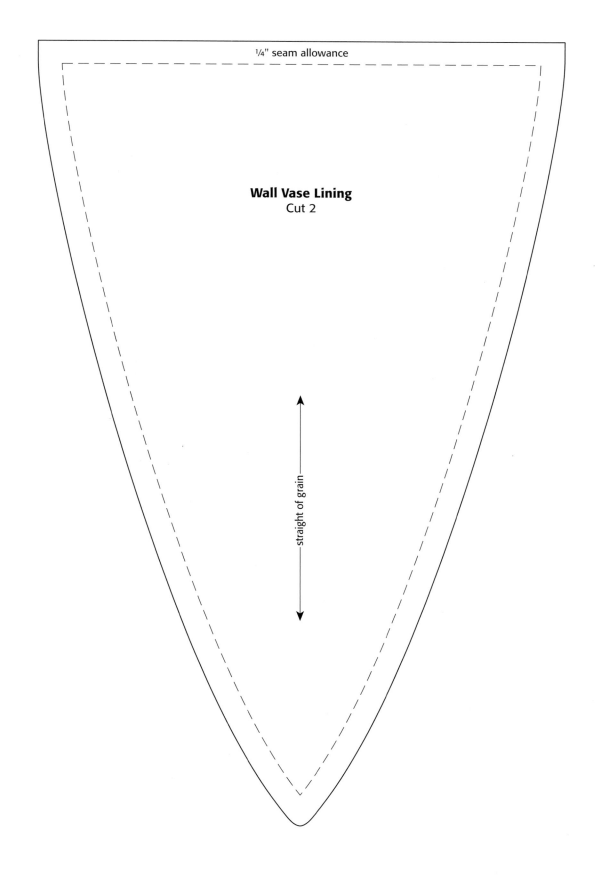

¼" seam allowance

Wall Vase Lining
Cut 2

straight of grain

MUSICAL TABLE RUNNER

This table runner, in the shape of a musical staff, features some Italian words that are used to indicate the speed and mood of a piece of music. It would look great on top of an upright piano—just change the measurements for a custom fit. The finished table runner shown measures 14" x 44".

Materials

(42"-wide fabric unless otherwise noted)

NOTE: The artwork used in this table runner can be found on pages 70–72.

> 10 June Tailor printer fabric sheets
> 1½ yds. light-colored fabric for middle panel of runner, ends, and backing
> 14" x 44" piece of low-loft batting
> Air-soluble marking pen
> Baby blue quilting thread
> Thread to match the light-colored fabric
> Glue stick

Prepare the Artwork

NOTE: Refer to "Preparing Artwork" on page 5.

PREPARING ARTWORK WITH A COMPUTER, SCANNER, AND PRINTER

Scan the artwork on pages 70–72 at 100 percent. Print out each of the 2 blue border panels 5 times, 1 per page. On 8 of these pages, fit 1 of the word appliqués; you will need 2 of each of the 4 words. Allow the printed fabric to dry. Rinse as suggested in "About the Printer Fabric" on page 5.

PREPARING THE ARTWORK WITH A PHOTOCOPIER

Copy the artwork on pages 70–72 at 100 percent onto the printer-fabric sheets. You will need 5 copies of both blue border panels. They should be arranged 1 per page. Include 1 of the word appliqués on 8 of the pages; you will need 2 of each of the 4 words. Allow the printed fabric sheets to dry. Rinse as suggested in "About the Printer Fabric" on page 5.

Cutting

From the light-colored fabric, cut:
> 1 rectangle, 6½" x 40½", for the middle panel
> 1 rectangle, 14½" x 44½", for the backing
> 2 rectangles, 2½" x 14½", for the end pieces

From the printer fabric, cut:
> 5 border panels, 4½" x 8½"
> 8 word appliqués, cutting around the outer edges of the artwork

Making the Table Runner

1. Make the top and bottom borders by stitching 5 of the blue panels together along the short edges.

2. Sew the top and bottom borders to the 6½" x 40½" center panel; press the seam allowances toward the borders only if your central panel is a very light color.

3. Sew the 2½" x 14½" end pieces, right sides together, to the short ends of the runner top; press the seam allowances toward the runner.

Copy the bracket pattern on page 72 at 200 percent. Mark the bracket shape on the end pieces of the runner; trim the fabric along the outer marked line.

4. Mark 5 lines, 1" apart, starting 1" from the edges of the blue border, on the center panel; do not include the end pieces. Mark the quilting lines on the end brackets as indicated on the pattern.

5. Pin-baste the runner top to the batting (See "Layering and Basting" on page 10.) Quilt along the marked lines with baby blue quilting thread. Also quilt in the ditch along the seam where the end pieces are joined to the quilt top. Trim the batting along the outer edge of the bracket on the short sides.

6. Prepare the word appliqués by folding the corners over diagonally and then turning the ¼" seam allowances to the wrong side; secure with dabs of glue stick. Arrange along the center of the runner as shown in the quilt plan on page 69; secure with a dab of glue stick. Position five words facing in one direction, and five in the opposite direction. Use an appliqué stitch to secure them to the runner: Thread a needle with about 18" of thread; knot 1 end. Insert the needle into the seam allowance on the back of the piece, then bring it to the front along the fold line. Bring the needle straight off the fabric and insert into the background; move the needle forward about ⅛" under the background fabric (work from right to left if you are right-handed, and left to right if you are left-handed). Bring the needle up to the right side of the fabric, at the edge of the appliqué, catching only a few threads of the appliqué. Continue along all the edges.

7. Pin the quilted runner top to the 14½" x 44½" piece of backing fabric with right sides together. Trim the short ends of the backing fabric to match the table runner top. Sew ¼" from the edge all around, leaving an 18" opening on 1 of the long sides. Turn the runner right side out; slipstitch the opening closed.

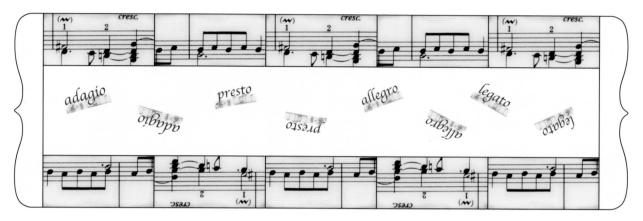

Quilt Plan

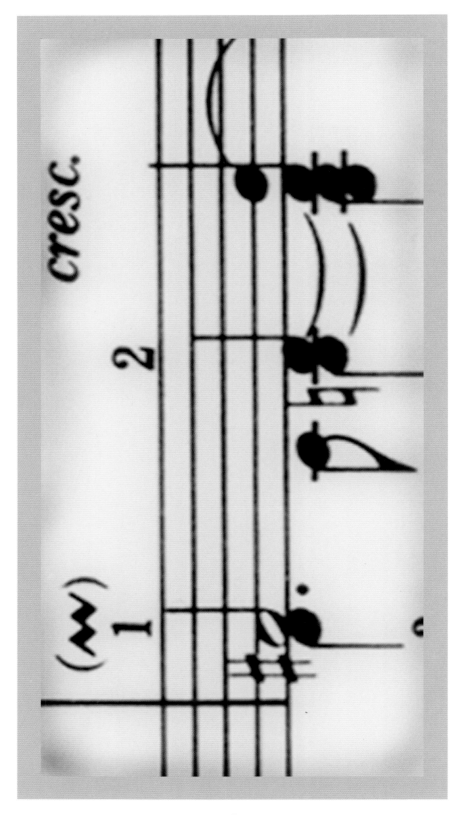

Border 1

Border 2

Appliqués

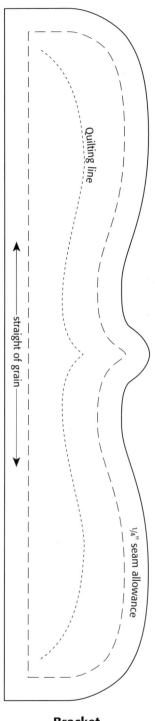

Bracket
Enlarge pattern 200%.

BIRD WALL HANGINGS

This pair of bird wall hangings uses only 2 sheets of printer fabric, and can be made in an afternoon. If you choose some of the other animals from the clip art source we used, try making your own custom border art to match. Each wall hanging measures 7" x 8½".

Materials

(42"-wide fabric unless otherwise noted)

NOTE: The bird images used for these wall hangings are from *286 Full-Color Animal Illustrations from Jardine's Naturalist's Library* by Sir William Jardine, published by Dover Books (see "Sources" on page 96 of this book). The border artwork can be found on pages 75 and 76 of this book.

2 June Tailor printer fabric sheets
2 pieces of low-loft batting, at least 7" x 8½"
2 pieces of muslin, at least 7½" x 9",
    for backing
Blue quilting thread to match blue border
Off-white thread
12" ribbon, ¼"-wide, for hanging loops
2 sheets off-white paper, 8½" x 11"
Permanent fabric glue
Glue stick

Prepare the Artwork

NOTE: Refer to "Preparing Artwork" on page 5.

PREPARING ARTWORK WITH A COMPUTER, SCANNER, AND PRINTER

Using the book mentioned in the Note above, scan the birds at the bottom of page 38 (*Trochilus cyaneus* and *Nectarina phoenicura*). Size the images to be about 6" tall, then paste each of them into 5½" wide x 7" tall files. Print out on a piece of off-white paper and then scan the image again. Scan the border art on pages 75 and 76 of this book at 100 percent and paste the birds into the borders, making sure the outer edges of the art are aligned with the inner edges of the photo corners. Print one image per sheet of printer fabric; allow to dry. Rinse as suggested in "About the Printer Fabric" on page 5.

PREPARING THE ARTWORK WITH A PHOTOCOPIER

Using the book mentioned in the Note at left, copy the birds at the bottom of page 38 (*Trochilus cyaneus* and *Nectarina phoenicura*) onto off-white paper; size them to be about 6" tall. Cut a 5½" x 7" piece from each bird paper, with the birds centered within. Copy the border art on pages 75 and 76 of this book at 100 percent, and glue the birds into the center, using a glue stick; be sure the edges are aligned with the photo corners. Copy 1 image per sheet of printer fabric; allow to dry. Rinse as suggested in "About the Printer Fabric" on page 5.

Making the Wall Hangings

1. Baste a piece of batting to the wrong side of both pieces of printer fabric, using a basting glue stick; be sure that the entire image is backed. On each piece of fabric, machine-quilt a border along the outer and inner edges of the blue border, using blue quilting thread. Do not quilt around the photo corners.

2. Pin the muslin backing to the printer fabric, right sides together. You will see the edges of the image through the muslin; mark the stitching line on the muslin ¼" inside the outer edges of the image underneath. Stitch along this line, leaving about 5" at the bottom for turning. Turn right side out; press. Slipstitch the opening closed.

3. Cut the ribbon into 2 pieces, each 6" long. Fold the ends under ⅛" and secure with permanent fabric glue. Fold the ribbons in half to form a loop; then center and attach the ribbon ends flat against the back of each hanging with permanent fabric glue. The ends of the ribbons should be horizontally aligned, and the top of the loop should be ¼" from the upper edge of the wall hanging.

Frame 1

Frame 2

INFANT QUILT

This quilt, featuring friendly farm animals, created especially for this book, is the perfect gift for a baby shower. The finished quilt measures 29½" x 33½".

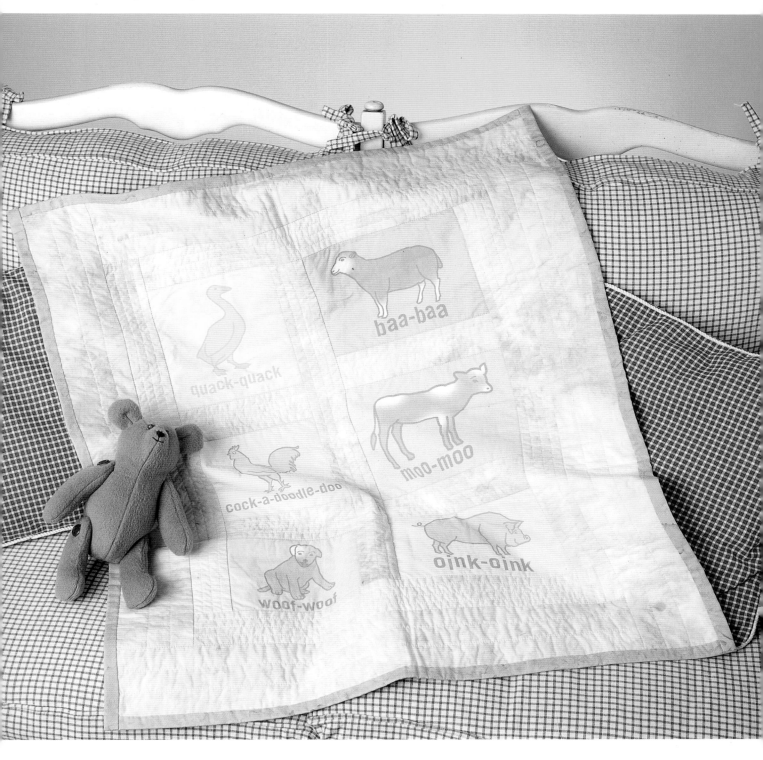

Materials

(42"-wide fabric unless otherwise noted)

NOTE: The artwork used in this quilt is by Biz Stone and can be found on pages 83–88.

6 June Tailor printer fabric sheets
1 yd. blue for backing and binding
1 yd. mottled pastel for the sashing and borders
30" x 34" piece of low-loft batting
Off-white quilting thread
Air-soluble marking pen

Prepare the Artwork

NOTE: Refer to "Preparing Artwork" on page 5.

PREPARING ARTWORK WITH A COMPUTER, SCANNER, AND PRINTER

Scan in the duck, rooster, cow, pig, sheep, and dog images on pages 83–88 at 100 percent. Print 1 image per sheet of printer fabric; allow to dry. Rinse as suggested in "About the Printer Fabric" on page 5.

PREPARING ARTWORK WITH A PHOTOCOPIER

Have the duck, rooster, cow, pig, sheep, and dog images on pages 83–88 copied at 100 percent, 1 image per sheet of printer fabric. Allow to dry. Rinse as suggested in "About the Printer Fabric" on page 5.

Cutting

From the blue fabric, cut:
1 rectangle, 32⅛" x 36⅛" for the backing, which will be folded to the front to make the binding.

From the mottled pastel fabric, cut:
2 pieces, 2½" x 7½" for the sashing
2 pieces, 2½" x 9½" for the sashing
1 piece, 2½" x 22½" for the sashing
2 pieces, 2¼" x 20¼" for the top and bottom inner borders
2 pieces, 2¼" x 24½" for the side inner borders
2 pieces, 4¼" x 26¼" for the top and bottom outer borders
2 pieces, 4¼" x 30¼" for the side outer borders

From the printer fabric, cut:
1 duck panel, 7½" x 7½"
1 sheep panel, 9½" x 6½"
1 rooster panel, 7½" x 6½"
1 cow panel, 9½" x 7½"
1 dog panel, 7½" x 5½"
1 pig panel, 9½" 5½"

Making the Infant Quilt

1. Piece together the duck, rooster, and dog vertically, using the two 2½" x 7½" sashing strips between the panels.

2. Piece together the sheep, cow, and pig vertically, using the two 2½" x 9½" sashing strips between the panels.

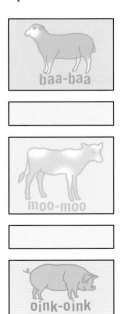

3. Stitch the 2 columns together vertically using the 2½" x 22½" sashing strip between; the duck should be on the left, and the sheep on the right.

4. Sew the 2¼" x 20¼" and the 2¼" x 24¼" border strips to the animal block counter-clockwise; begin with a 2¼" x 24¼" strip on the right side of the animal block. Align the top of the strip with the top of the animal block, letting 2¼" hang past the bottom. Stop stitching 4" from the bottom of the strip.

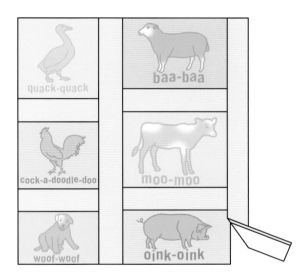

5. Next, add a 2¼" x 20¼" strip to the top, then the remaining 2¼" x 24¼" strip to the left side, and finally the last 2¼" x 20¼" strip to the bottom. With the right-hand strip folded out of the way, sew the bottom strip across the animal block; then fold the right-hand strip back down and sew it in place.

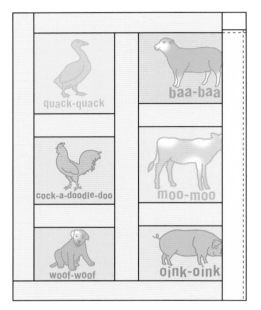

Attach the right side first, then the top, then the left, and finally the bottom.

6. Using the 4¼" x 26¼" strips and the 4¼" x 30¼" strips, add the outer border in the same way as the inner border. Use the longer strips for the sides and the shorter strips for the top and bottom of the quilt.

7. With an air-soluble marking pen, mark 3 lines ½" apart on the sashing and inner borders. On the 4" outer borders, mark 2 lines 1" apart, starting 1" from the inner edge of the border. Layer the quilt top over the batting. Pin-baste every 3" to 4" (see "Layering and Basting" on page 10). Quilt in the ditch along all seams (see "Machine Quilting" on page 11). Quilt on the marked lines.

8. Pin the backing fabric to the quilt top, wrong sides together, allowing 1⅛" extra fabric along each edge. Sew ¼" away from the edge of the quilt top to secure the backing fabric.

9. Fold the backing fabric over ½" to the front and press, starting with the top and bottom, then the sides.

Then fold the fabric over snugly against the edge of the batting, again starting with the top and bottom, then the sides, and press. Slipstitch the binding down. Secure the corners with a few stitches where the fabric folds meet.

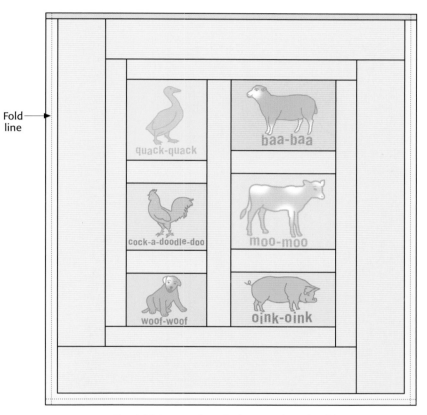

First fold the top, then the bottom, then the sides.

Instructions for this project begin on page 78.

Sheep

cock-a-doodle-doo

Rooster

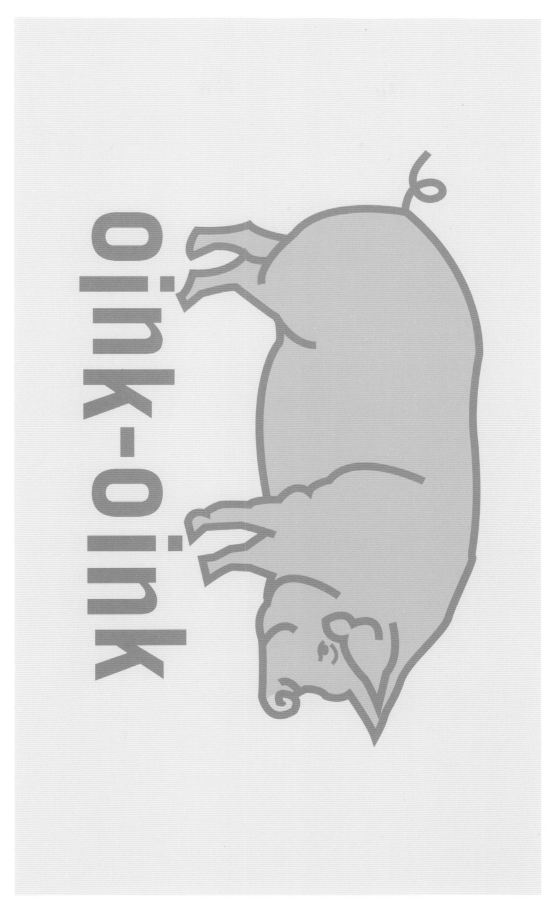

Pig

Duck

Dog

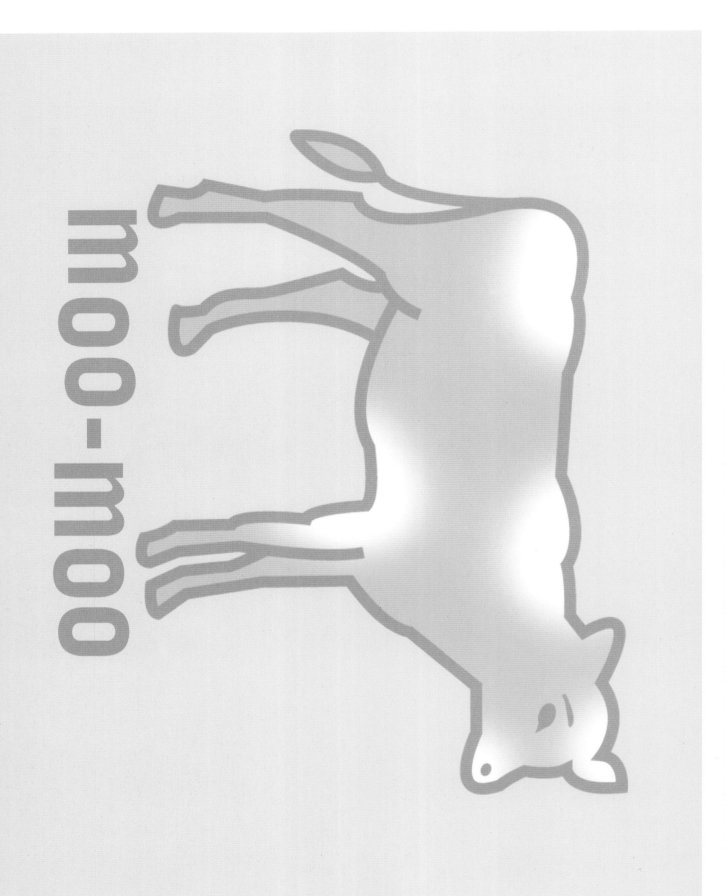

Cow

INDIAN LAP QUILT

This project features quilted traditional Indian henna designs with floral themes that complement the brightly-colored, nature-inspired Indian folk art. With many paintings to choose from, you can personalize your quilt by choosing the animals or colors you like best, or you could explore the variety of henna designs to come up with your own unique patterns. The finished quilt measures 42" x 40".

Materials

(42"-wide fabric unless otherwise noted)

NOTE: The artwork for this project is taken from *Authentic Folk Designs from India in Full Color* by K. Prakash, published by Dover Books.

> 10 June Tailor printer fabric sheets
> 1 yd. yellow fabric for borders
> 2½ yds. muslin for sashing and corner squares
> 1¼ yds. 45"-wide low-loft batting
> Off-white and yellow quilting thread
> If preparing artwork with a photocopy machine, colored paper to match the outer edges of the artwork
> Air-soluble marking pen

Prepare the Artwork

NOTE: Refer to "Preparing Artwork" on page 5.

PREPARING THE ARTWORK WITH A COMPUTER, SCANNER, AND PRINTER

Using *Authentic Folk Designs from India in Full Color* (see Note above), scan the elephant image on page 22, the image with 2 birds on page 16, and the larger snake on page 20. Size each image to fit within a 6"-wide x 4"-tall file. Then create 4 new files that measure 6½" x 4½" and color them to match the outer edges of the three pieces of art, either by scanning colored paper or filling the background with a color on your computer. Copy and paste the artwork into these files. Flip the elephant to face in the opposite direction for the fourth file.

Print 2 pieces of art to a page. You can do this by creating a new file 6½" wide x 9" high, copying the finished artwork, and pasting 2 images into the new file. Print 1 page of each

elephant for a total of 4, 5 pages of birds for a total of 10, and 3 pages of snakes for a total of 6. Allow the printer fabric sheets to dry. Rinse as suggested in "About the Printer Fabric" on page 5.

PREPARING ARTWORK WITH A PHOTOCOPIER

Using *Authentic Folk Designs from India in Full Color* (see Note at left), size the animals to fit within a 6" x 4" space. Have the art color copied 2 times, then ask the for the elephant to be flipped so that it faces in the opposite direction and copy 2 additional times. Paste each animal, 2 per page, onto a piece of 8½" x 11" colored paper to match the outer edges of the images. Copy 1 page of each elephant for a total of 4, 5 pages of birds for a total of 10, and 3 pages of snakes for a total of 6. Allow the printer fabric to dry. Rinse as suggested in "About the Printer Fabric" on page 5.

Cutting

From the yellow fabric, cut
> 4 squares, 2½" x 2½" for the inner border
> 2 strips, 4¼" x 32½" for the side outer border
> 2 strips, 4¼" x 34½" for the top and bottom outer borders
> 5 strips, 2" x 42" for the binding

From the muslin, cut:
> 4 squares, 4¼" x 4¼" for the outer border
> 5 strips, 2½" x 28½" for the sashing and the side inner borders
> 16 strips, 2½" x 6½" for the sashing
> 2 strips, 2½" x 30½" for the top and bottom inner borders
> 1 piece, 46" x 44" for the backing

From the batting, cut:
  1 piece, 46" x 44"

From the printer fabric sheets, cut:
  20 animal images, each 6½" wide x 4½" tall

Making the Indian Lap Quilt

1. Piece together the first and last columns of the quilt, using 8 of the 2½" x 6½" sashing strips, all the elephants, 4 birds, and 2 snakes.

First column   Last column

2. Piece together the middle 2 columns of the quilt, using the remaining 2½" x 6½" sashing strips and the rest of the animals.

Make 2.

3. Use the 2½" x 28½" sashing strips to join the columns together. Stitch a 2½" x 28½" strip to each side of the pieced quilt for the side inner borders.

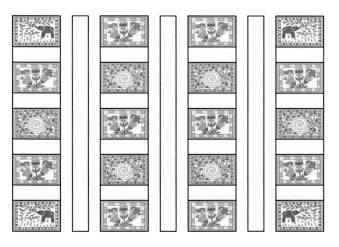

4. Sew 2 of the 2½" yellow squares to the short ends of one of the 2½" x 30½" inner border strips; repeat with the remaining 2½" yellow squares and the remaining 2½" x 30½" inner border strip. Sew the top and bottom inner border strips to the quilt.

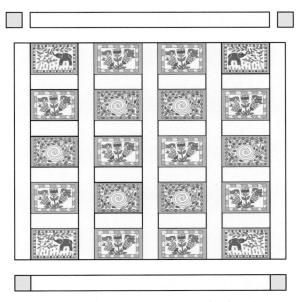

Sew the 2½" squares onto the inner border strips before sewing them to the quilt center.

5. Sew the 4¼" x 32½" yellow border strips to the left and right sides of the quilt, then sew 2 of the 4¼" muslin squares to the short ends of one of the 4¼" x 34½" yellow strips. Repeat with the remaining 4¼" muslin squares and the remaining 4¼" x 34½" yellow strip to make the top and bottom outer borders. Sew the outer border strips to the top and bottom to the quilt.

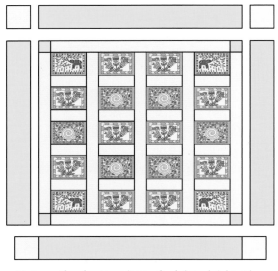

First sew the shorter strips to the left and right sides.
Then sew the 4¼" squares to the longer strips
before completing the border.

6. Enlarge the quilting patterns on page 95 by 400 percent. Copy the quilting designs on page 94 at actual size. For the larger patterns on the border and long sashing strips, copy the pattern in sections and tape them together to make a complete pattern. Using tape, secure the patterns to a work surface (refer to the quilting guide for placement), then tape the quilt top in place. Trace the lines with an air-soluble marking pen. The fabric should be light enough to do this without the aid of a light box.

7. Layer the quilt top, batting, and backing. The batting and backing should extend 2" beyond the edges of the quilt top. Pin-baste the layers together every 3" to 4" (see "Layering and Basting" on page 10). Using

thread of coordinating color, machine-quilt along the marked pattern lines using free-motion quilting (see "Machine Quilting" on page 11). Trim the batting and backing even with the edges of the quilt top.

8. Join binding strips to make a continuous length. Trim 1 end at a 45-degree angle and fold ¼" to the wrong side. Fold the strip in half lengthwise, wrong sides together; press.

Fold line

9. Pin the binding to the quilt top, matching raw edges. Stitch ¼" from the raw edges, starting about 2" from the beginning of the binding. Stop stitching ¼" from the corner. Fold the binding up, then fold it back down, aligning the raw edges of the binding with the next side of the quilt. Begin stitching off the edge of the quilt top at the fold in the binding, ¼" from the edge along the next side.

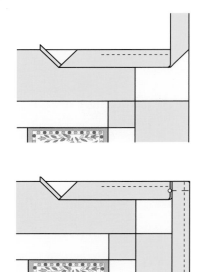

Continue to stitch binding around the remainder of the quilt in the same manner. Insert the end of the binding into the fold at the starting point; trim excess.

10. Turn the binding to the back of the quilt, covering the stitching line and creating a miter at each corner; slipstitch in place.

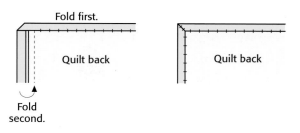

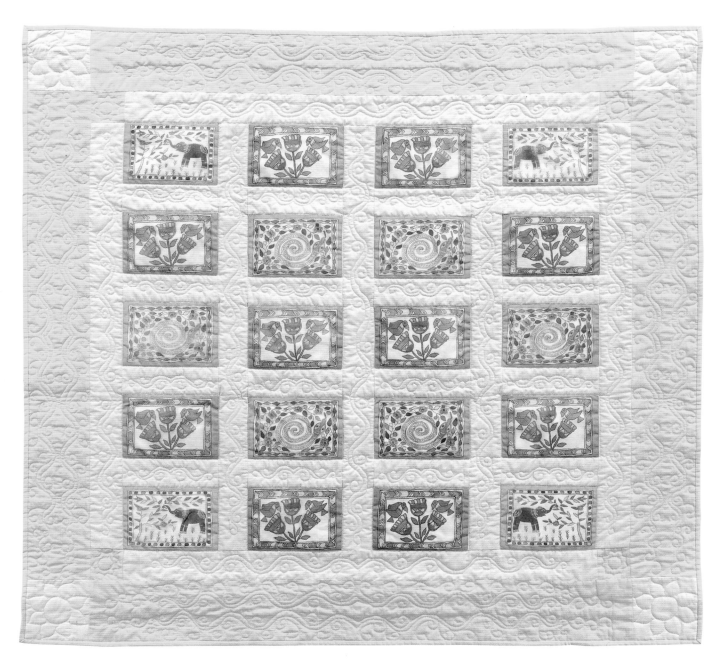

Quilting Diagram

2" squares

4" squares

Top eight 2" x 6" sashing strips

Bottom eight 2" x 6" sashing strips

Indian Lap Quilt
Quilting Designs

Patterns are actual size. Do not enlarge.

Top and bottom
30" strips
(point should
face "out")

Left and right
28" strips
(point should
face "out")

Middle
28" strip

Side borders

Top and bottom
borders

Indian Lap Quilt
Quilting Designs

Enlarge patterns 400%.

Sources

DOVER PUBLICATIONS, INC.
31 East 2nd Street
Mineola, NY 11501-3582
Tel.: (516) 294-7000
Fax: (516) 742-6953

Request their Pictorial Archive Catalog, which features over 800 books of artwork for use by craftspeople.

NOTE: Dover doesn't currently have a web site, but their books and CD-ROMs are available through many online retailers, including www.arttoday.com, with whom they have an exclusive licensing agreement.

HANCOCK'S OF PADUCAH
3841 Hinkleville Road
Paducah, KY 42001-9155
Tel.: (800) 845-8723
www.Hancocks-Paducah.com

This company offers a multitude of fabrics for quilters, including the textured solids used throughout this book.

JUNE TAILOR
P.O. Box 208
2861 Highway 175
Richfield, WI 53076
Tel.: (800) 844-5400
www.junetailor.com

Write or call for a product catalog or more information on the distribution of June Tailor products, which are available in many craft and quilting supply stores across the nation.

SHAMBHALA PUBLICATIONS, INC.
Mailing List
P.O. Box 308
Back Bay Annex
Boston, MA 02117
Tel.: (617) 424-0030
Fax: (617) 236-1563
www.shambhala.com

Write to Shambhala Publications for a catalog which includes their Agile Rabbit Editions. All the books in this series feature royalty-free artwork for craftspeople, and include a companion CD-ROM so you don't have to scan the images yourself.

LIVIA MCREE

You can refer to www.liviamcree.com for sources and advice regarding the tools, supplies, and techniques used in this book.

About the Author

Photo courtesy of Douglas M. Bell

Born in Nashville and raised in New York City by her working artist parents, Livia McRee has always been within a creative sphere. Her interest in writing led her to an editorial position with *Handcraft Illustrated* magazine, where she became a featured designer. Focusing on home decorating, sewing, and other arts for *Handcraft Illustrated* prepared Livia for a career in craft design and writing.

More of Livia's how-to projects can be seen in publications such as *The Crafter's Project Book* (Rockport Publishers) and *Creepy Crafty Halloween* (Martingale & Company) and at Craftopia.com. Find out about upcoming publications, free projects, crafting advice, and more about the techniques and tools used in the book by visiting www.liviamcree.com.

ABOUT THE ARTIST

Biz Stone, who created some of the reproducible art in *Instant Fabric*, is a graphic artist and the creative director of Xanga.com. More about Biz and links to his design and illustration work can be seen at www.bizstone.com.